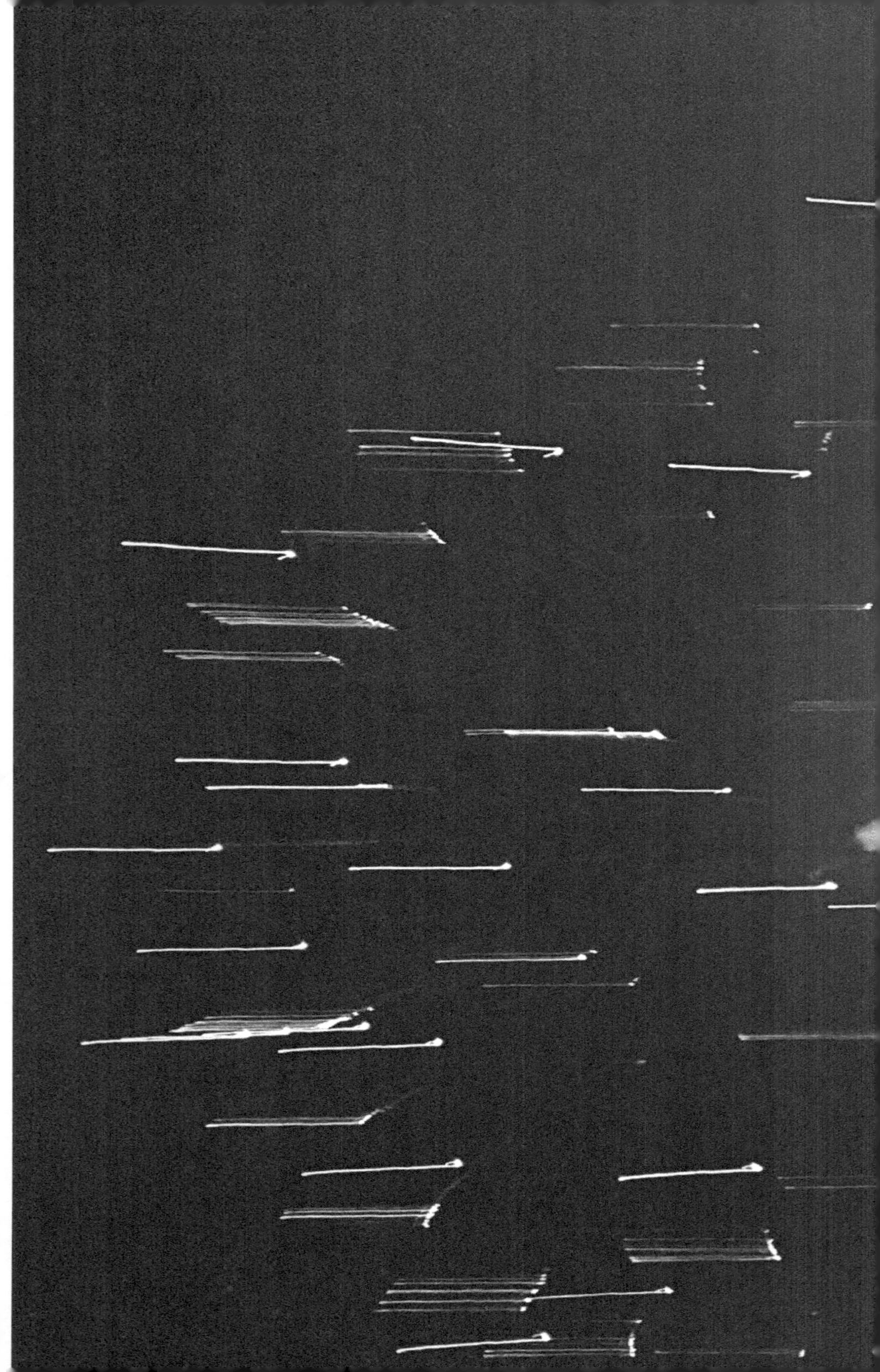

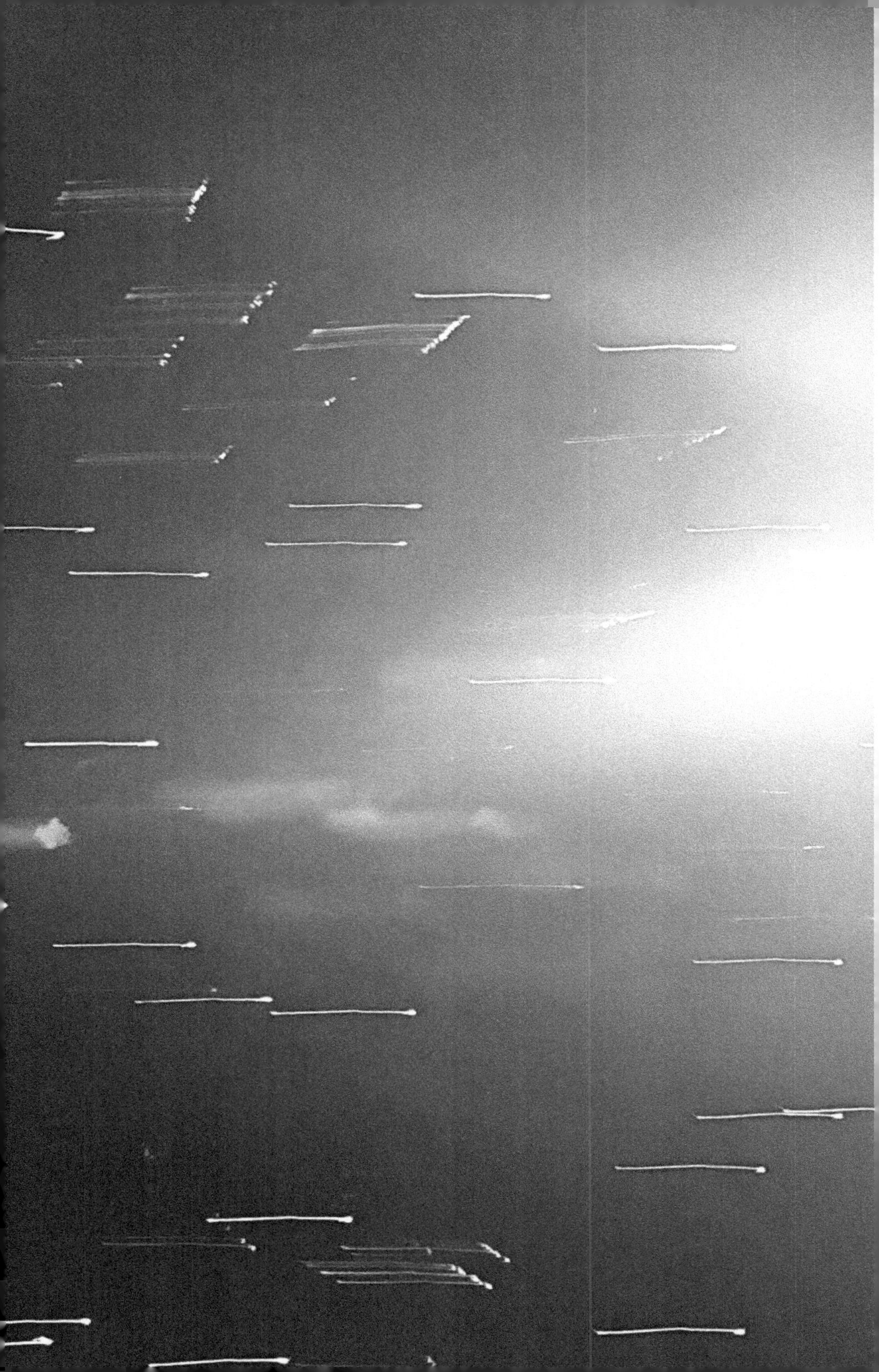

This is a work of creative nonfiction. Some parts have been fictionalized in varying degrees, and for various purposes.

First paperback edition August 2021

Book design by Ben C. Cunningham

Photography by Ben C. Cunningham

ISBN 978-1-7376750-0-6 (paperback)

ISBN 978-1-7376750-1-3 (ebook)

WWW.LEJARDIN.ONLINE

LE JARDIN

"A WALK THROUGH THE GILDED GARDENS"

BENJAMIN CUNNINGHAM

"DEDICATED TO THOSE WHO FIND THEM-SELVES LOST IN THE MOMENTS BETWEEN THE CRESTS AND TROUGHS OF THE HUMAN EXPERIENCE...

THAT SOME PEACE MAY BE FOUND IN READ-ING THE WORDS OF MY OWN STRUGGLE WITH SUCH."

"... AND DEDICATED TO MY MOTHER, FATHER, AND GRANDMOTHER WHO SO GRACIOUSLY SUPPORTED ME THROUGHOUT WRITING THIS BOOK"

"A WALK THROUGH
THE GILDED GARDENS"

A WALK THROUGH MY GILDED GARDENS

I LIVE IN THE HOPE OF LOSING YOUR NAME ON A PASSING SIGN

ADVERTISING SOME SHITTY POETRY BOOK BY SOME WANNABE WRITER

WHO RAN TO A CITY OF LIGHT AND SOUND

THE ONLY PLACE

BRIGHT ENOUGH

LOUD ENOUGH

TO ELIMINATE THE POUNDING IMAGE OF YOU

THAT I PAINTED IN MY GARDEN

WHILE THE ROSES BECAME STAINED WITH GREY

WHEN IT RAINED I WATCHED YOU WASH AWAY

AS I DO NOW

WHEN I WATCH THE RAIN PLUMMET ONTO PASSING UMBRELLAS

ORANGE

RED

GREEN

BLUE

ALL THE COLORS I SAW WITHIN YOU

ALL THE COLOR THAT BLOSSOMED IN MY GILDED GARDENS

THE GARDENS WHERE I ONCE PAINTED YOU

THERE WAS NO SPARK EXCEPT FOR THE ONE TO LIGHT MY MATCH

WHICH I THREW ONTO THE GOLDEN FOLIAGE

BURYING A MOMENT OF MY PAST IN THE SEA OF FLAMES

IN THE SEA OF LIGHTS

IN THE CITY OF LIGHTS

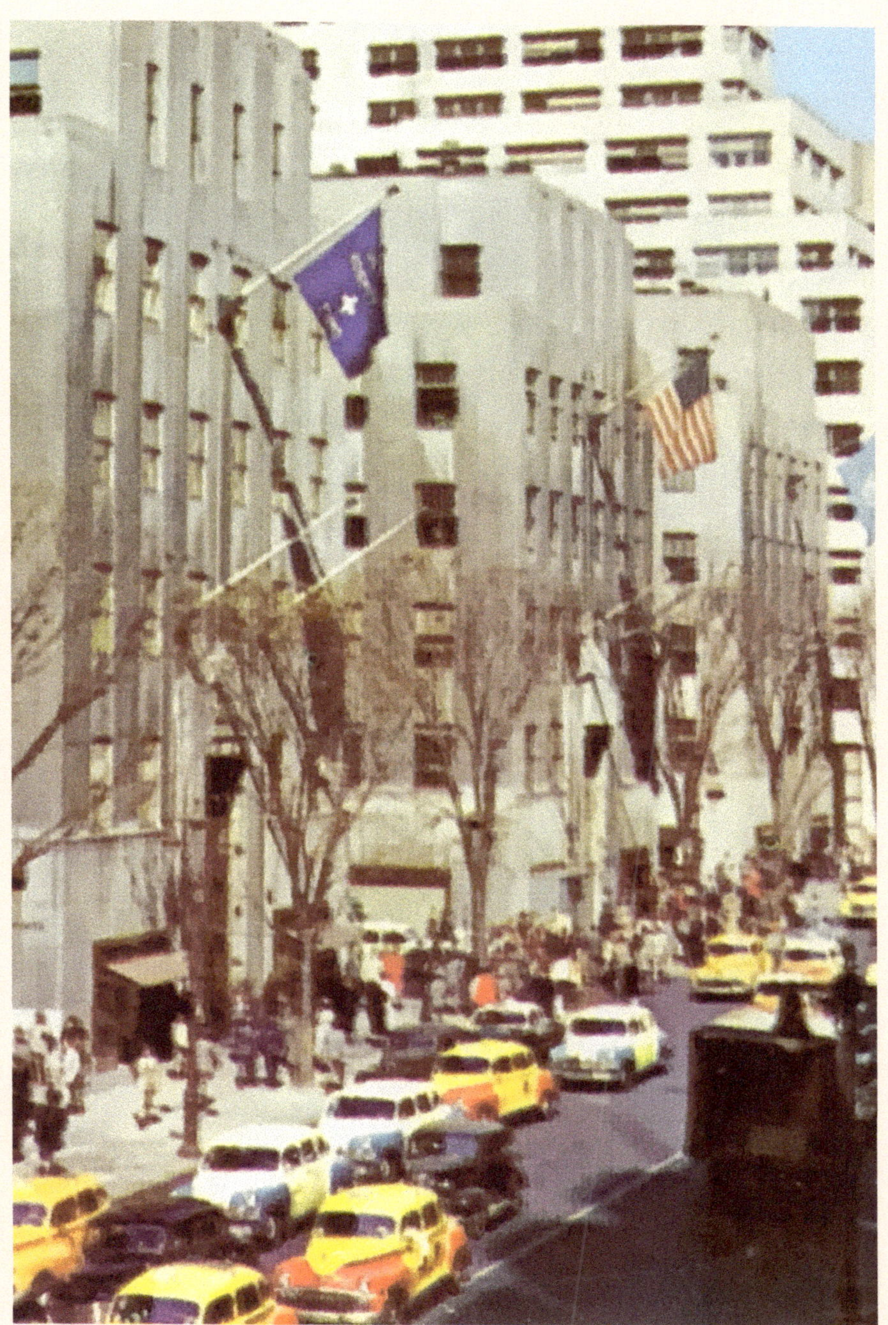

ITHACA

Ignoring my reality in upstate New York
Fleeing the entrapment of suburban living
In turn for some sort of rugged sense of duality
In the hills of Ithaca
The Greek city of Homer's creation
Where intellectuals converse over mediocre bagels and coffee

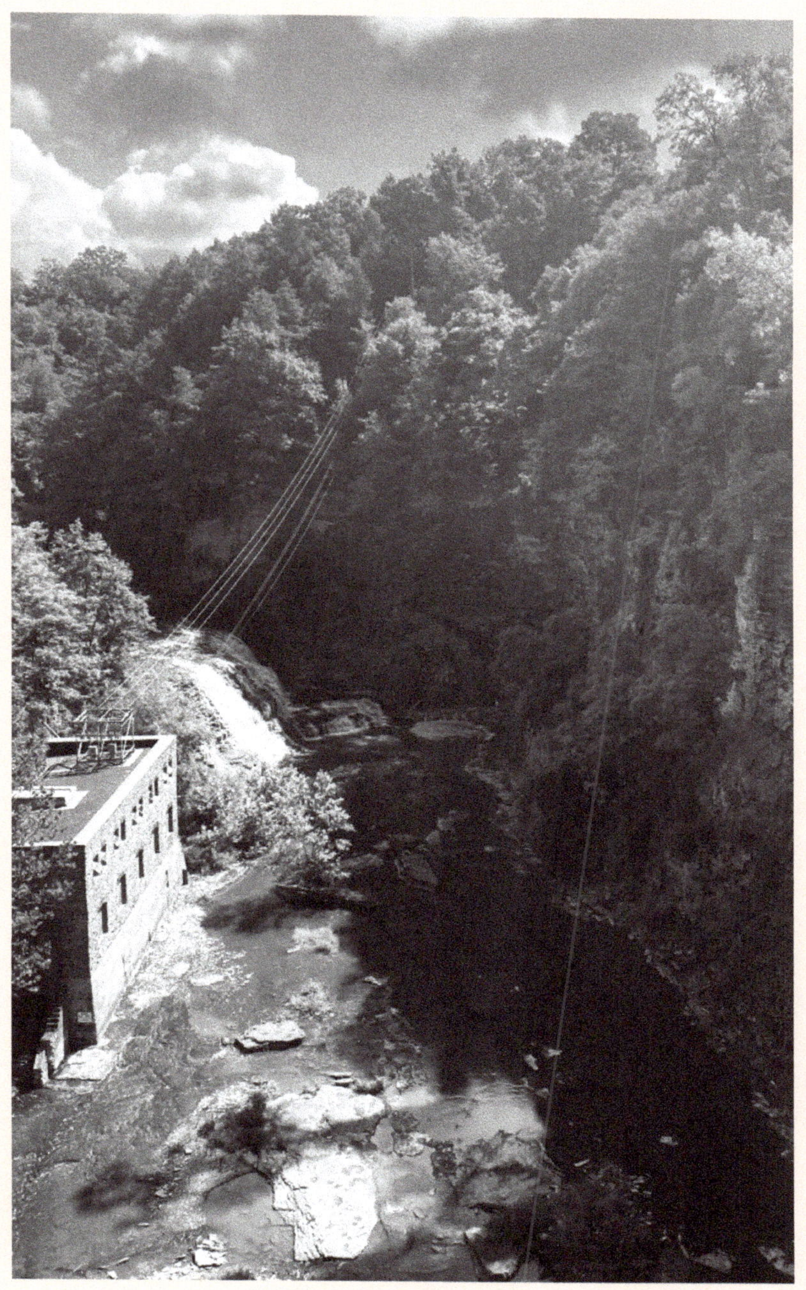

EXPLOSIONS AMONG THE ROSES

THEIR LOVE WAS GOLDEN
BURNED IN A GREAT LIGHT
BUT DIED WITH BROKEN CLOCKWORK AS THE FLOWERS BLOOMED IN SPRING…

THEY BOTH LIVED AND WANDERED WITHIN THE FLOWER GARDENS OF THEIR
MINDS
WHERE THEIR PATHS…
MET
CROSSED
DIVERGED
REPEATING A CYCLICAL STORY OF LOVES CONTINUOUS REBIRTH AND DEGRADA-
TION
SEEMINGLY UNEXPLAINABLE LOVE
YOUNG AND IMPOSSIBLE…

LIGHTING AN INDICA IN THE AIR OF MAY
WHEN THE WIDE-EYED, FRECKLED GIRL WAS BORN
WHO WORE THE EMERALD EMBROIDERED DRESS
AND WHO HELD AN UNDENIABLE TRUTH IN WHICH I WATCHED YOU CONTINU-
OUSLY DENY
HER FRAGILITY SHATTERED AND SHE WATCHED YOU SET FIRE TO HER WORLD
THE EXPLOSIONS IN THE ROSE GARDENS SHE BUILT FOR YOU
AND IN CERTAIN MOMENTS, HERSELF
THE GARDENS WHERE SHE DREAMED TO FIND YOU…

SHE LIVED IN THE RUINS OF DESTRUCTION IN THE GARDENS OF SOME FARAWAY
PLACE
UNSURE OF REALITY'S PRESENCE
SURROUNDED BY MASS DESOLATION
SHE WATCHED THE BROKEN CLOCK
AS THE HANDS TICKED IN HER MIND, DANCING BEHIND THE CRACKED SAPPHIRE
GLASS

THORNS AND ROSE PETALS SURROUNDING HER
AND SHE WAITED
AND SO I WATCHED...

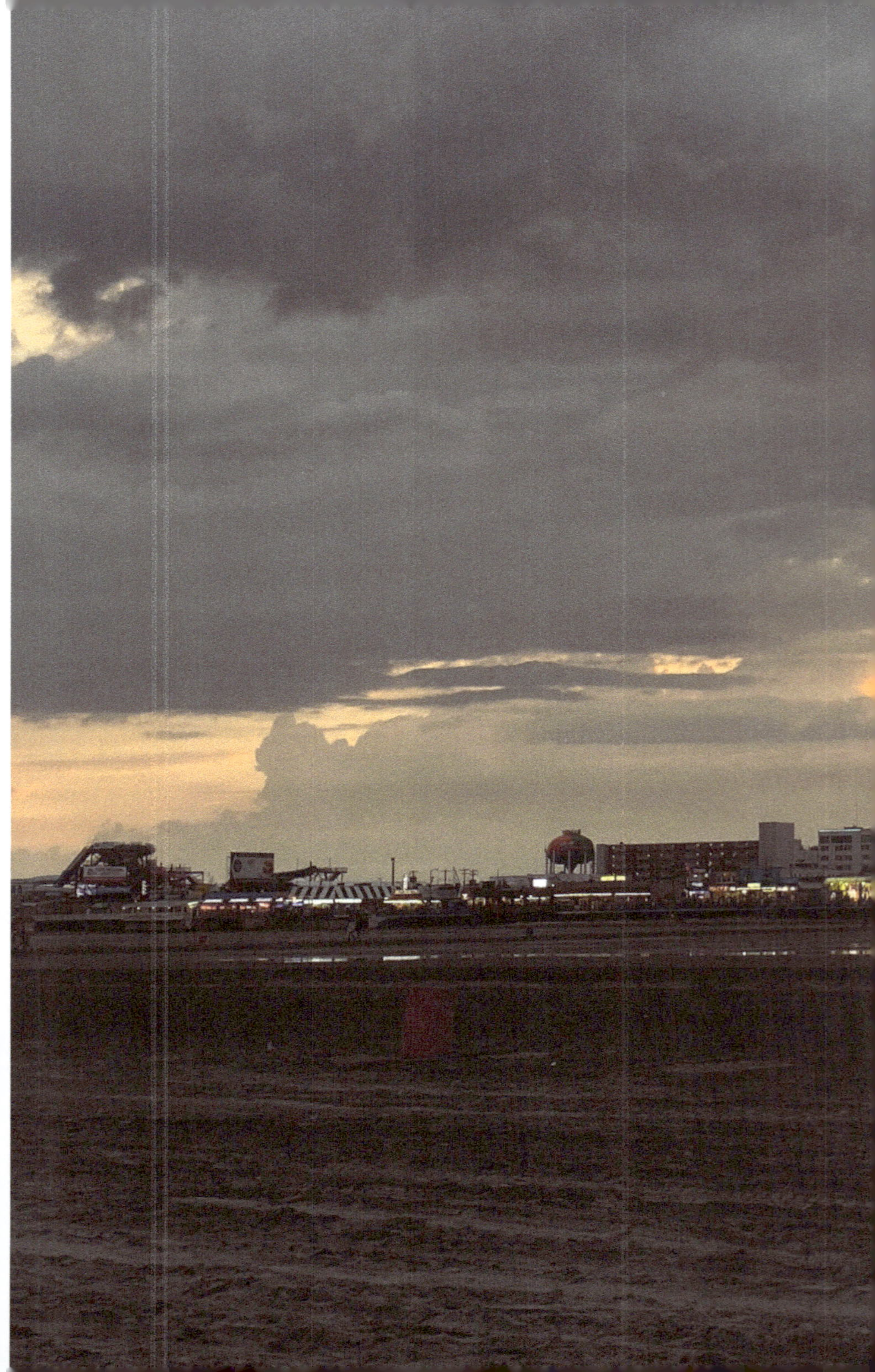

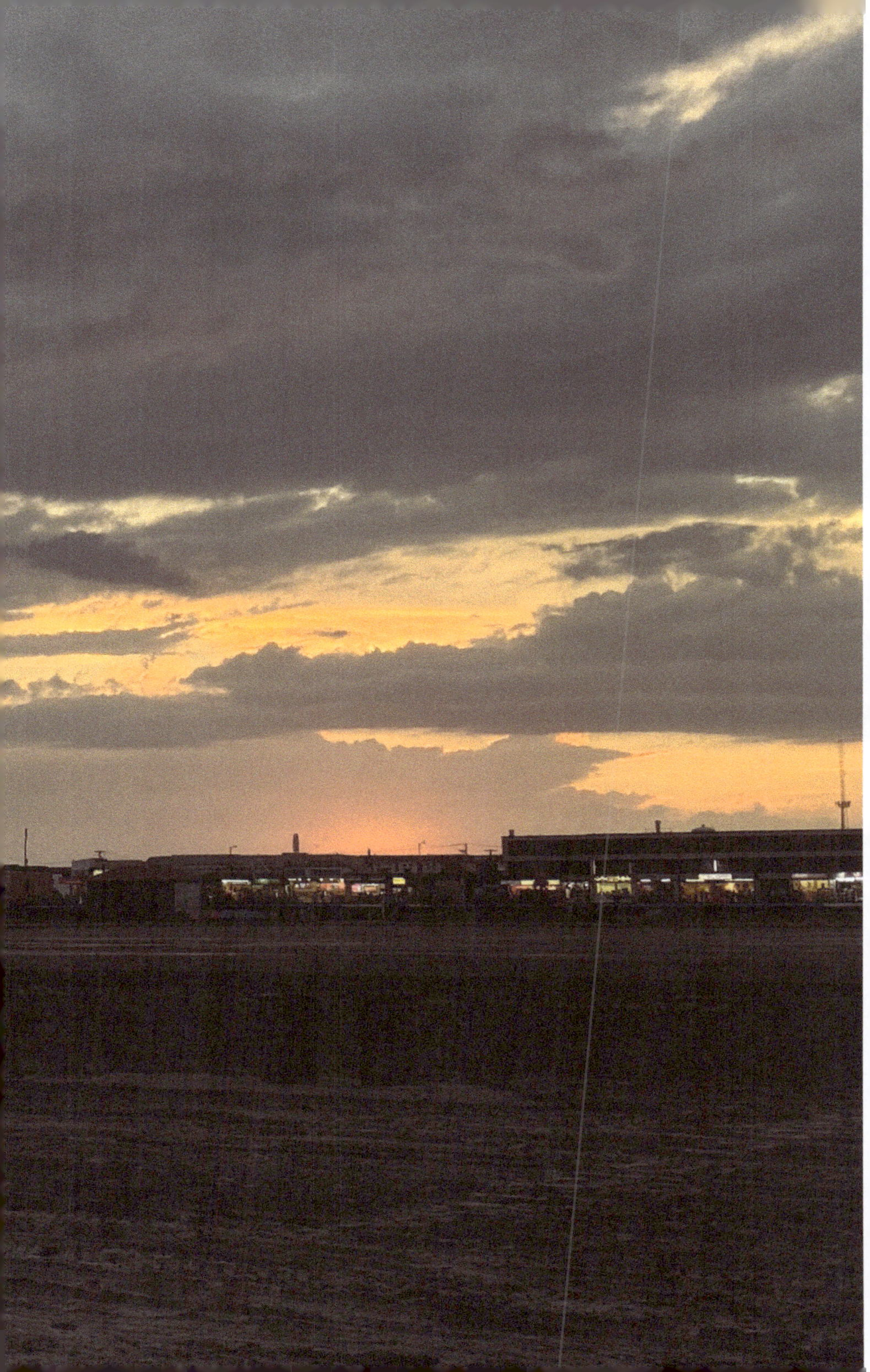

THOUGHTS FROM THE BEDFRAME

Silent blue skies dotted with puffs of white

A declaration of spring's arrival

As flowers bloom in an array of pastels

And the birds sing in the early morning

A chill breeze blows through the crack of the golden window

Fluttering the photos of past memories

Each a piece of my world

My definition

On these days I ponder my future

Aware of my past

The people of my life

The writers of my story

Where will the timeline continue?

And where will it end?

The sun shines bright

The air remains cool

Incense burns

Streams of smoke wisp through my room

Awakening a revolution of olfaction

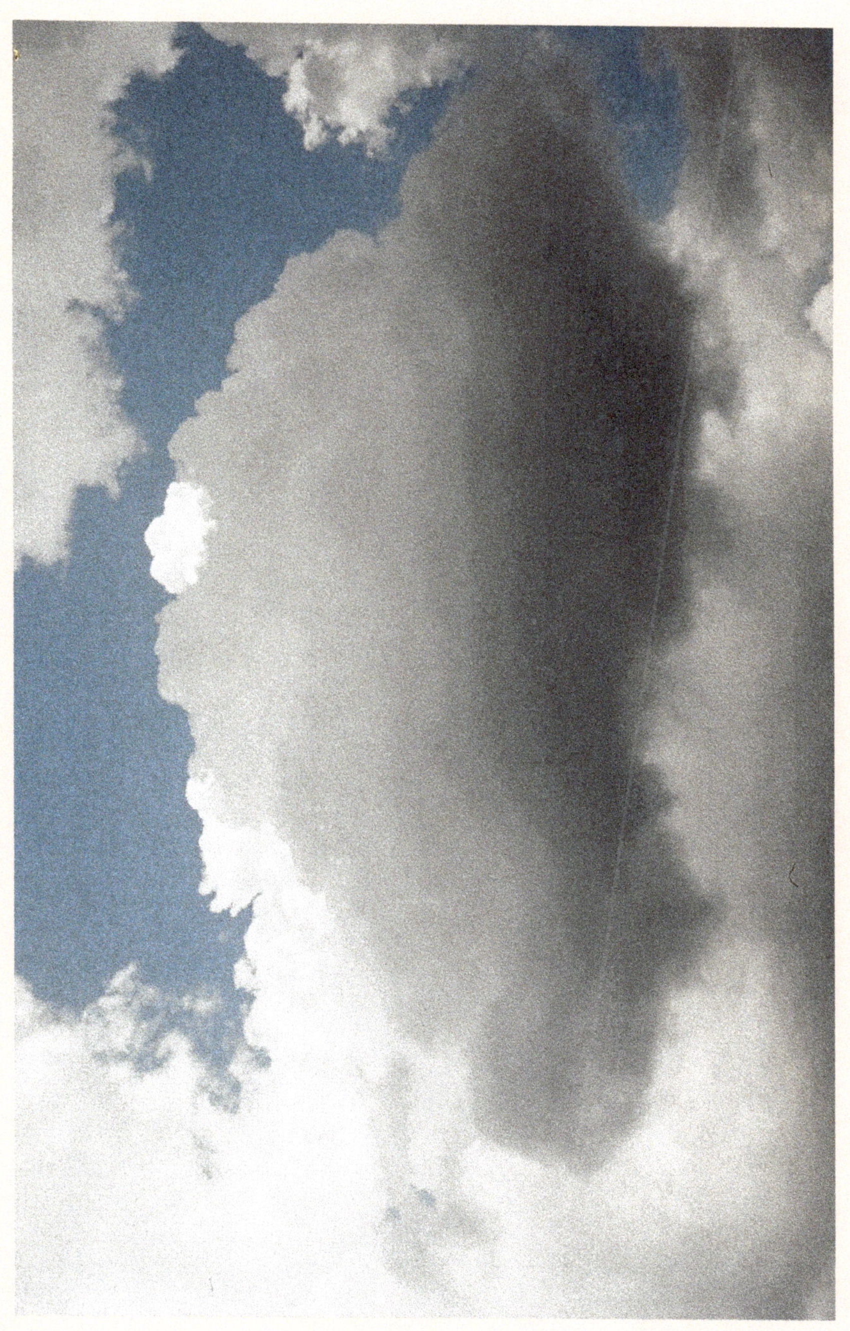

SO I HEARD YOU LIKE ART...

I WOULD PAINT ANYTHING ON CANVAS TO IMPRESS YOU
THOUSANDS OF BRUSH STROKES BUILDING THE STARS IN A SKY OF MAKE-BELIEVE
THE GOLDEN WHISPS ABOVE THE TINY TOWN
WHERE I FOUND CONTROL AT EASE
WHERE I DON'T SULK IN THE ENVY OF NOT HAVING YOU
OF NOT BEING WANTED BY YOU

I'LL SHOW YOU MY SILVER ETCHINGS.
LIKE DA VINCI
MY EMOTIONS UNLEASHED IN A FRENZY
LIKE KLINE
MY SEARCH FOR TRANQUILITY
LIKE MARTIN
WHATEVER IT TAKES TO MAKE YOU LOOK ONCE MORE
TO MAKE YOU IN AWE OF SOMETHING BY MY HAND
BUT YOUR BLIND IN MY DIRECTION
EVEN THOUGH I CRY IN COLOR AND SCREAM IN LIGHT

THOUGH I STILL PAINT WITH THE HOPE OF YOUR GAZE
UPON THE SURREALISM OF OUR UNKNOWN STORY
THAT EXISTED ONLY IN A WORLD WHERE THE CLOCKS MELTED AT HALF-PAST
ONE.

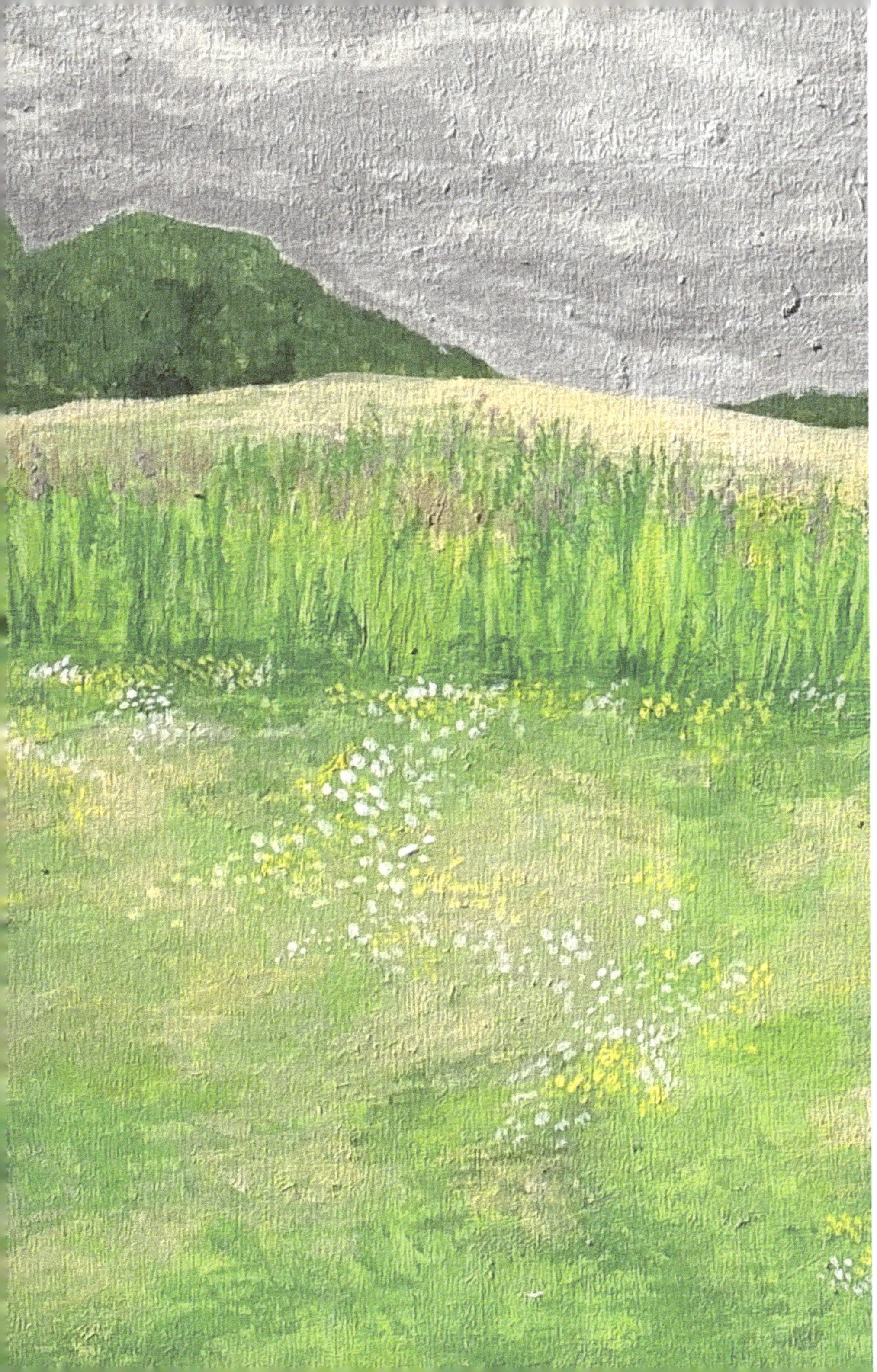

WHITE DRESS AND WHITE SAND

My mind wanders far outside the boundaries of my bedroom walls
To a place of temporary peace
Where serenity wears a white dress
And strolls the beaches of a coastline
In another world beyond human comprehension
Where I found peace with you
With your existence without me

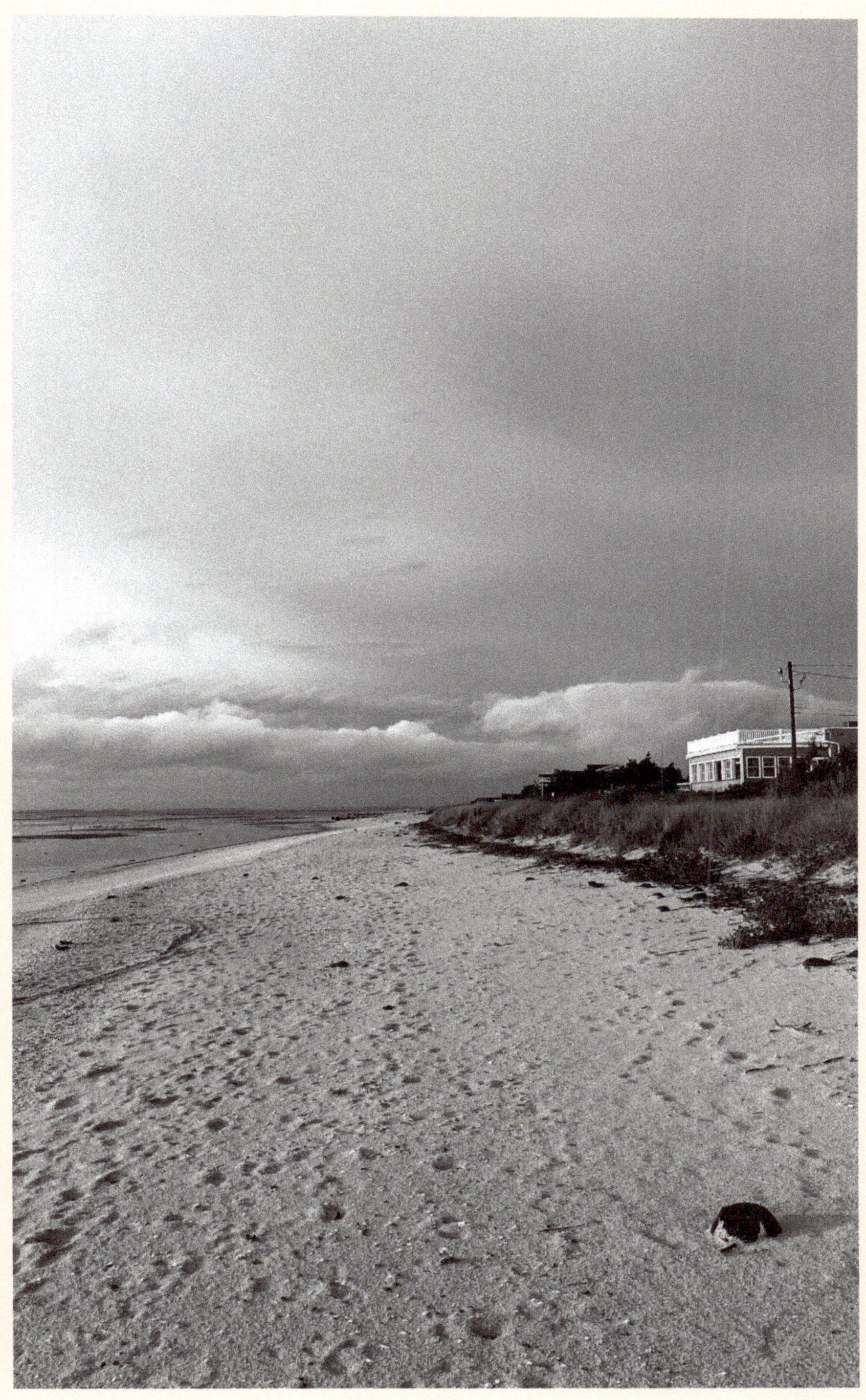

THE GARDENS OF GETHSEMANE

I think it's funny how fast I can forget you

When I get some kind of attention

Some sort of touch that isn't your own

My entire fantasy of the two of us

Vanishes before me

Healing wounds

Relieving Pain

Easing Sorrow

I questioned my liking for you

Was it your looks?

Or dreamt up personality that I created in my view of perfection

But I find myself with sharp cracks lining my sides

A potential to break into a million pieces when left alone

As the thought of no hand to hold or breath to hear becomes violent

The cries of string instruments playing in the spring sun

The beauty and violence intertwined within me

The violence that stabs back with my broken pieces

The beauty that paints your portrait with the blood that falls from

your ear

From a wound, I cannot heal

For your deceit and all of which I wanted to believe broke my porce-

lain defense

Until there's nothing

Not a word

Not a thought

Not a glance

Between us.

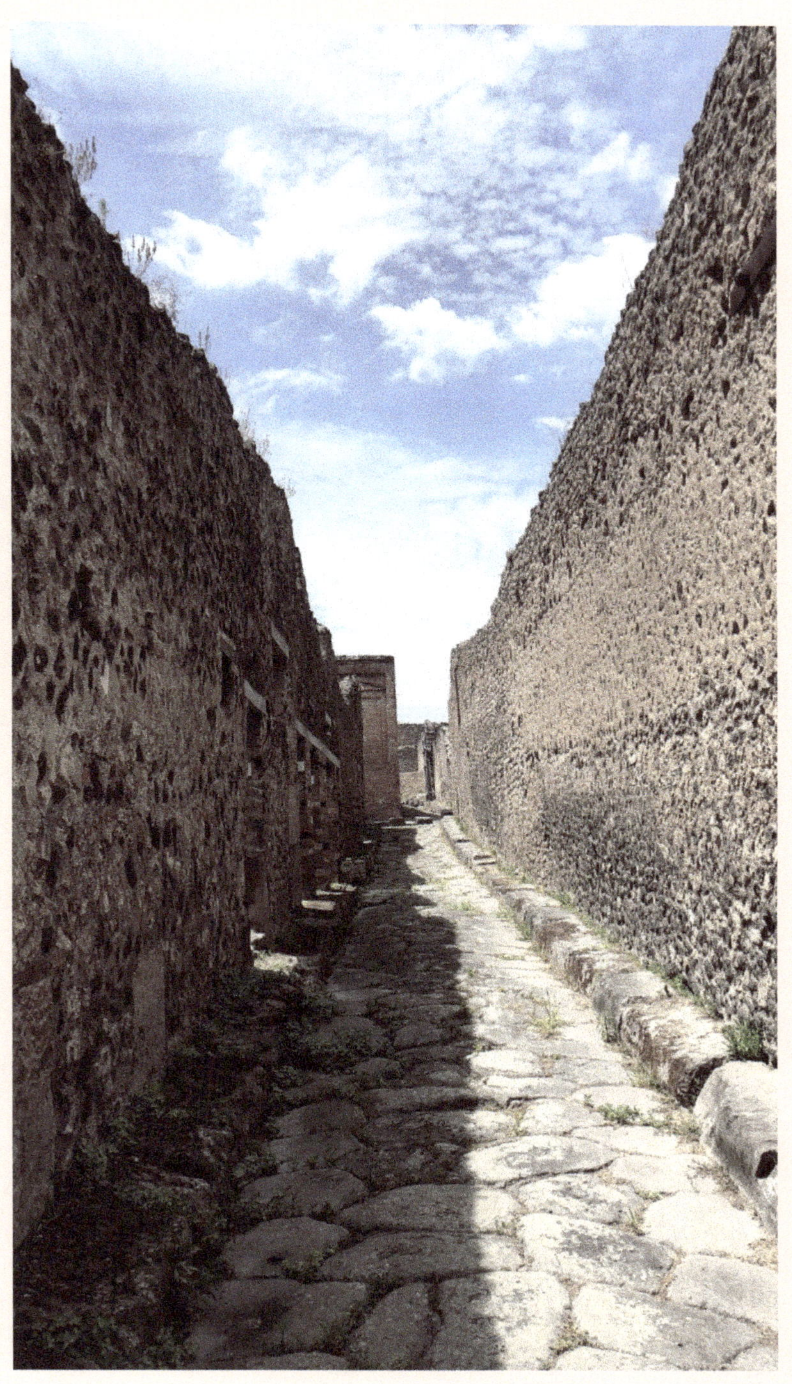

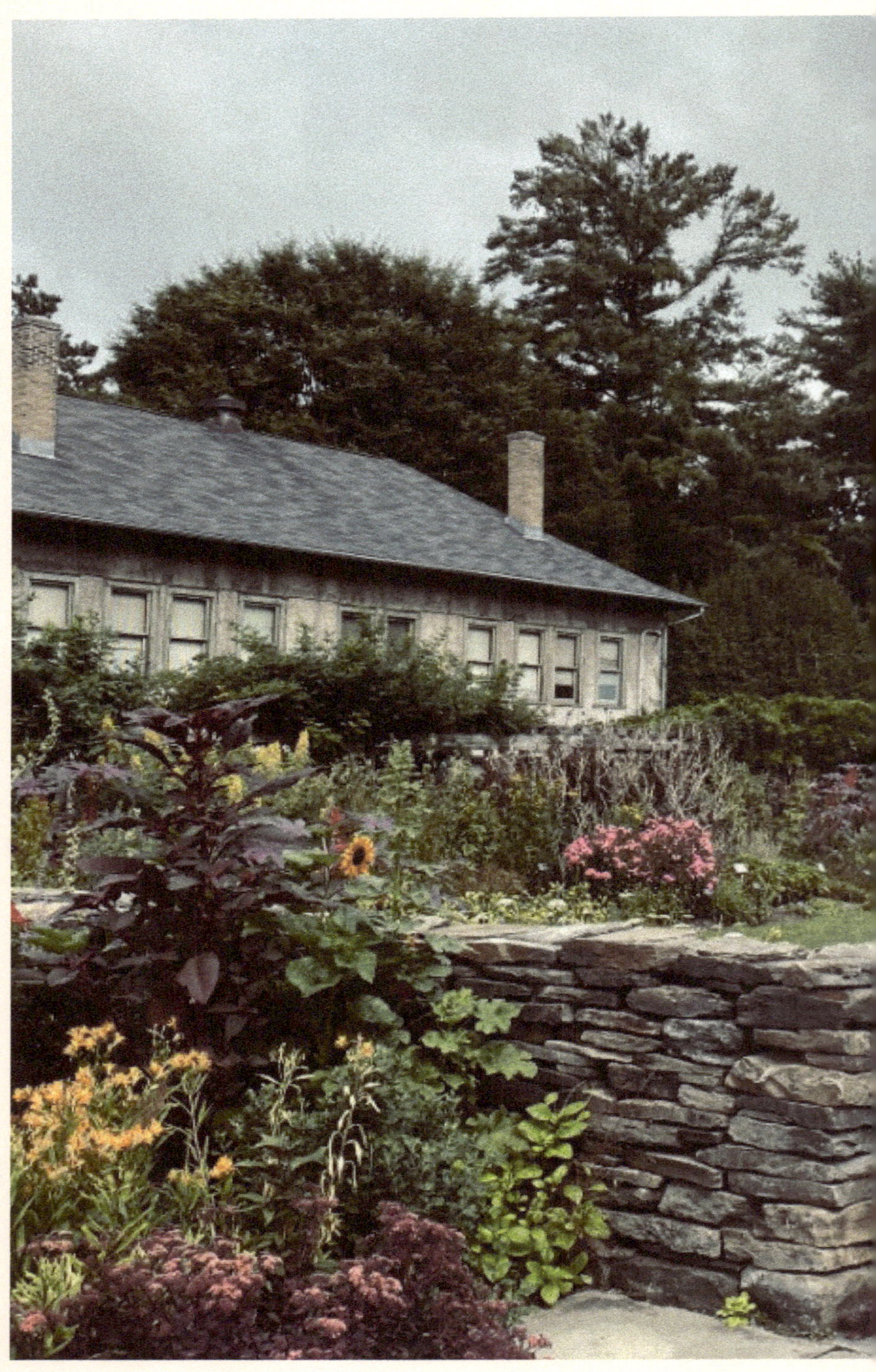

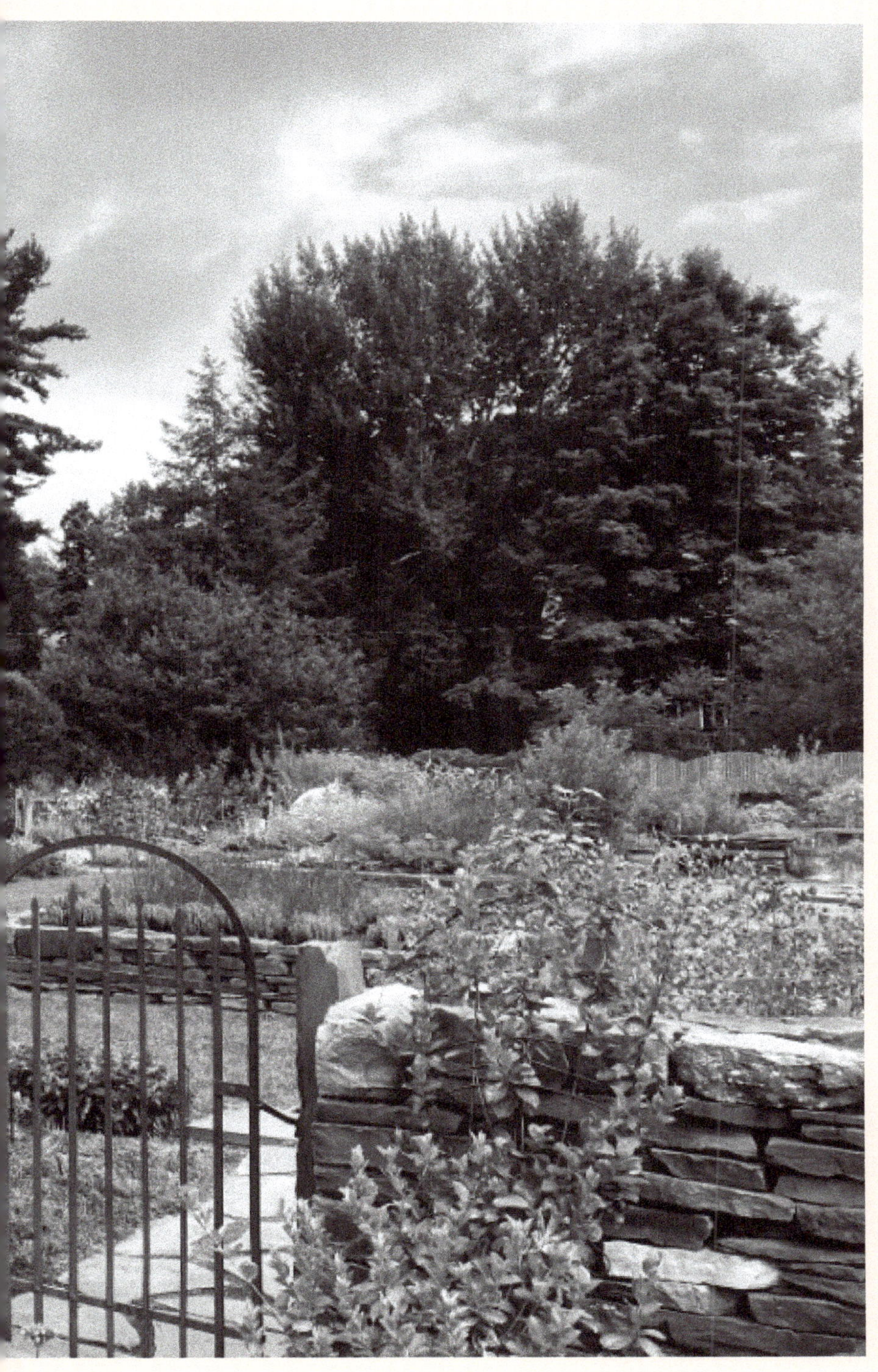

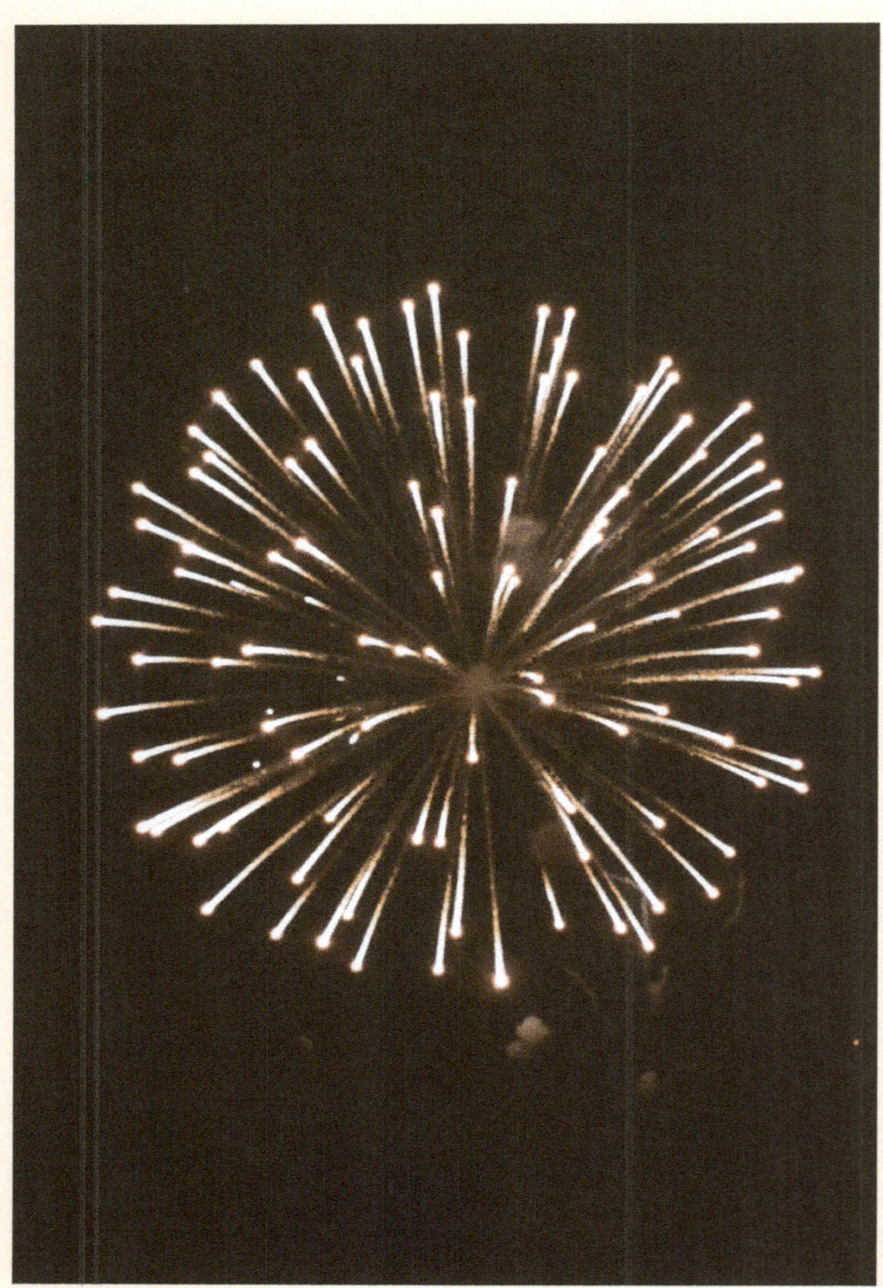

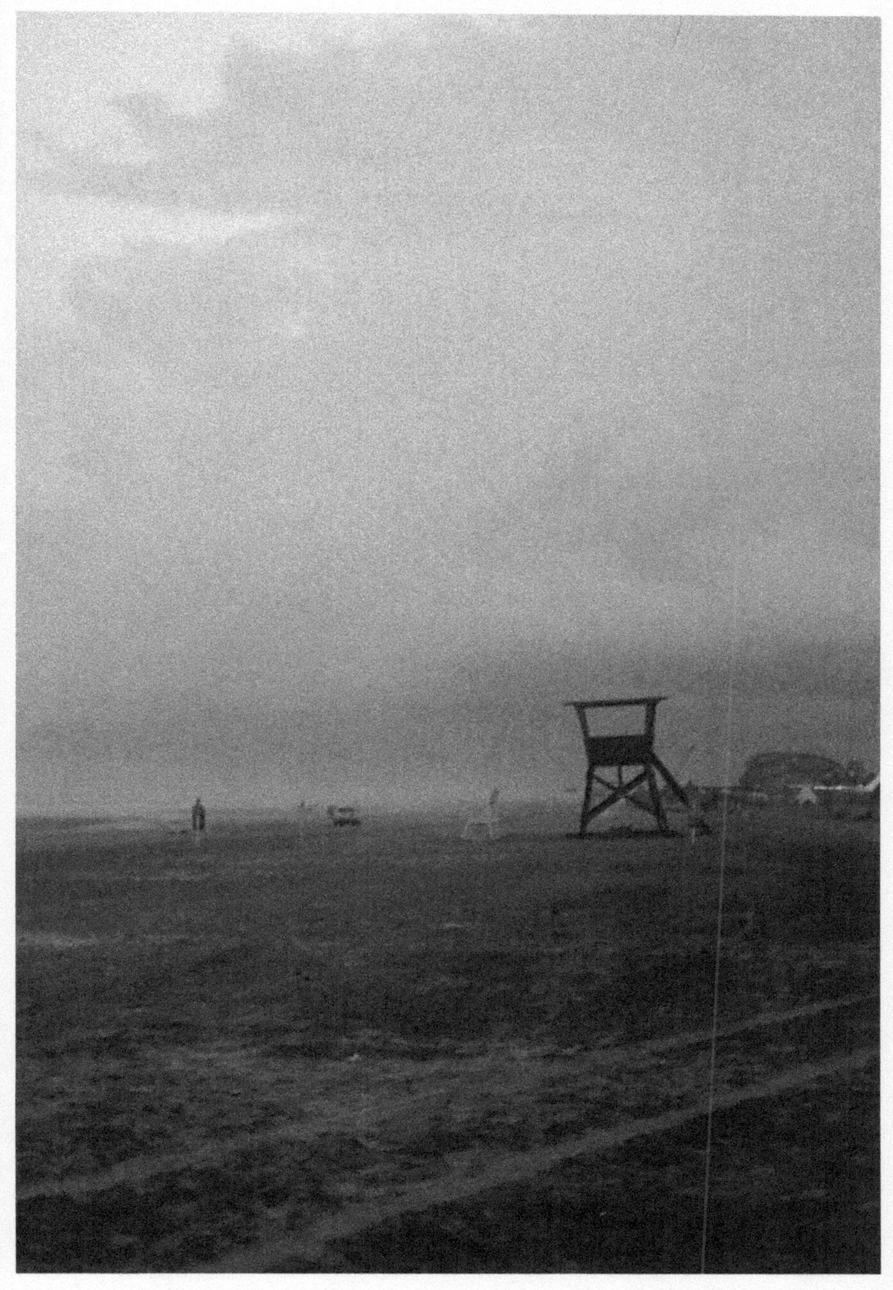

GOODNIGHT MOON

THE MOON GLISTENED FAR ABOVE THE SHORT GREY BUILDINGS OF A MEDIO-
CRE TOWN
REVEALING HERSELF TO THOSE BELOW
REMOVING HER SILK DRAPES
THE CLOUDS DEPARTED
THE CITY STREETS SHINED BRIGHT
MAILBOXES STOOD IN THE NIGHT
SILENTLY
LIKE SOLDIERS MADE TO DEFEND
THE VIEW FROM THE CAR WINDOW WAS MINUTE ON MY SCALE OF EMOTION
THE WORLD WAS AT PEACE BUT I COULD NOT BE
TEARS FELL, WITH RAPID FORCE
SO I SAT AND HELD MY EYES SHUT
UNTIL THE DARKENED WORLD DISAPPEARED INTO THE VAST BEAUTY OF
NOTHINGNESS
THE TREES HAD WAVED TO ME
THE MOON HAD SHED A TEAR
OR SO MY DAD HAD SAID
THE DARKENED WORLD BECAME FULL OF LIGHT
A LIGHT THAT BURNED THE REALIZATION OF NO CONTROL INTO MY SKIN

The feeling of powerlessness
The thought of having nothing
The thought of being nothing
The bright light began to become comfort
Almost familiar
I walked the aisles of the dilapidated Walmart
Bathing in incandescence
Until I left the store and found the moon once more
So I wished the lady good night
As I had done as a child
Aware of her return the next day
But when I say goodnight to you now
I say it with anger
Hoping your light may never shine bright again

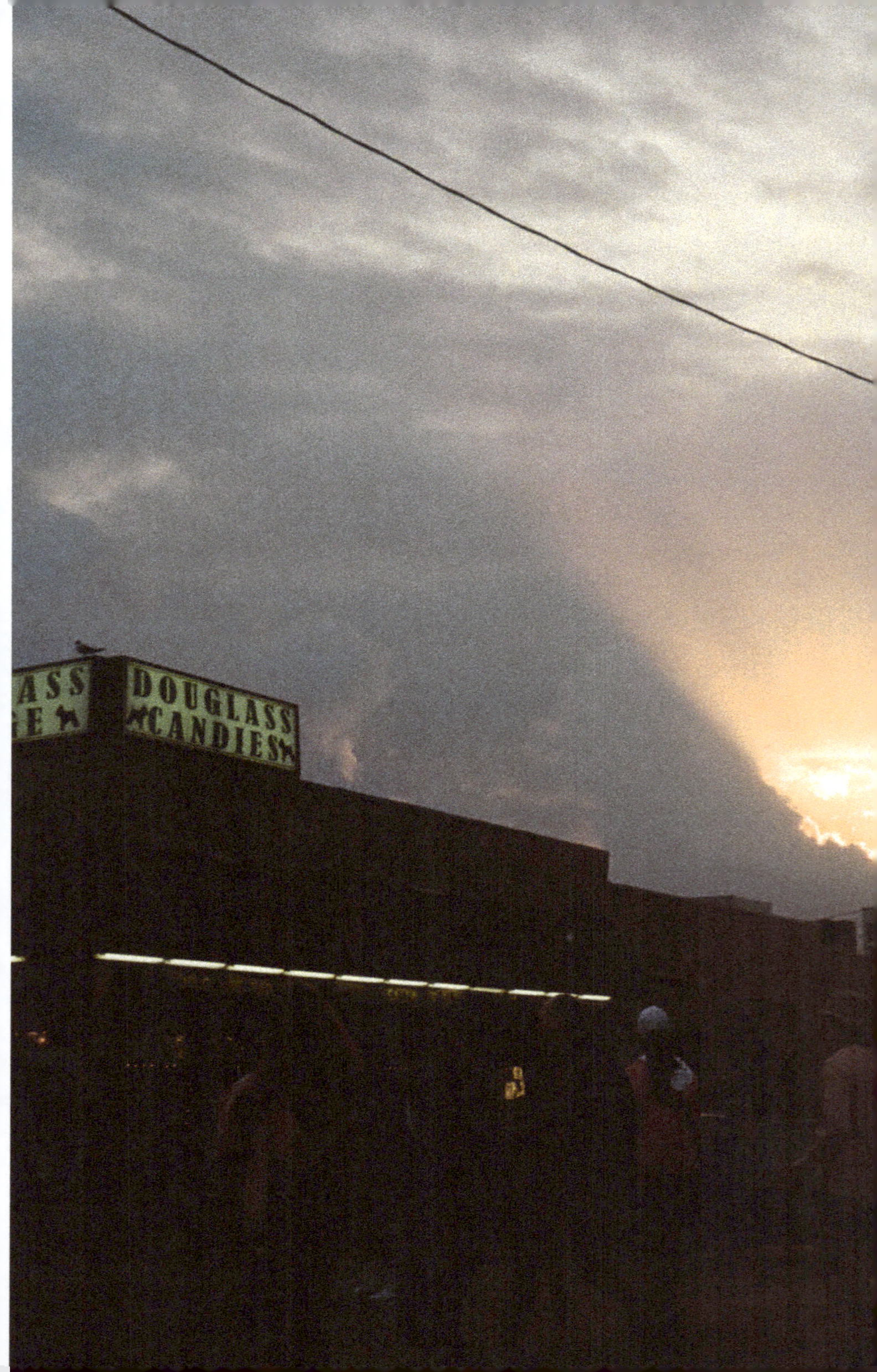
ASS
DOUGLASS
GE
CANDIES

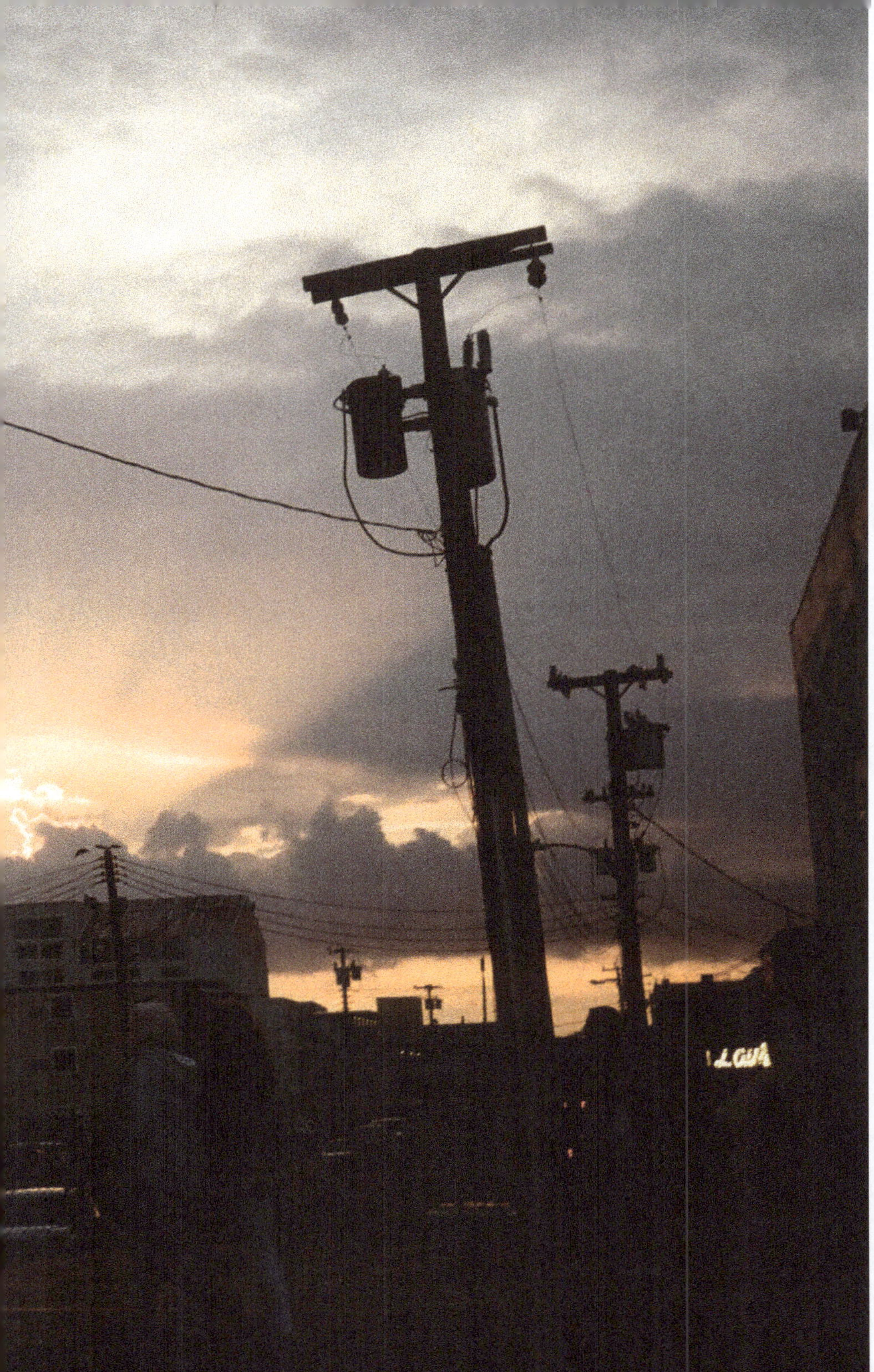

A FEW MILES PAST THE GARDENS...

She ran the coastline
Back and forth
Never knowing what was truly chasing her
Was it him?
Was it her?
Was it herself?
She didn't know
And neither did I
But she ran with such fear
So I watched
And painted the picture
With words on this page
The sun was bright
The sky was clear
The ocean was blue
I wish I could say that's all I knew
Her white dress blew in the coastal winds
Like the kite her father flew when she was young

The one she buried with him
With blood covered hands
The sky then turned dark
And her dress became stained wine red
From shared blood
Which poisoned her storyline
The skies thundered with each of her steps
Sand swirled in the air around her
The once gentle winds tore at her dress
Her serenity gradually stolen as the clock ticked
Counting down an end to a story that only lived on this
coastline
A few miles past the gilded gardens she once called
home…

She fled for freedom.
So I threw down pen and paper.
And I ran.

INTRUSIVE THOUGHTS

Burning down Buckingham Palace
Setting fire to every piece of artwork in the Louvre
The uncontrollable wandering of my mind
To a destination far beyond Timbuktu

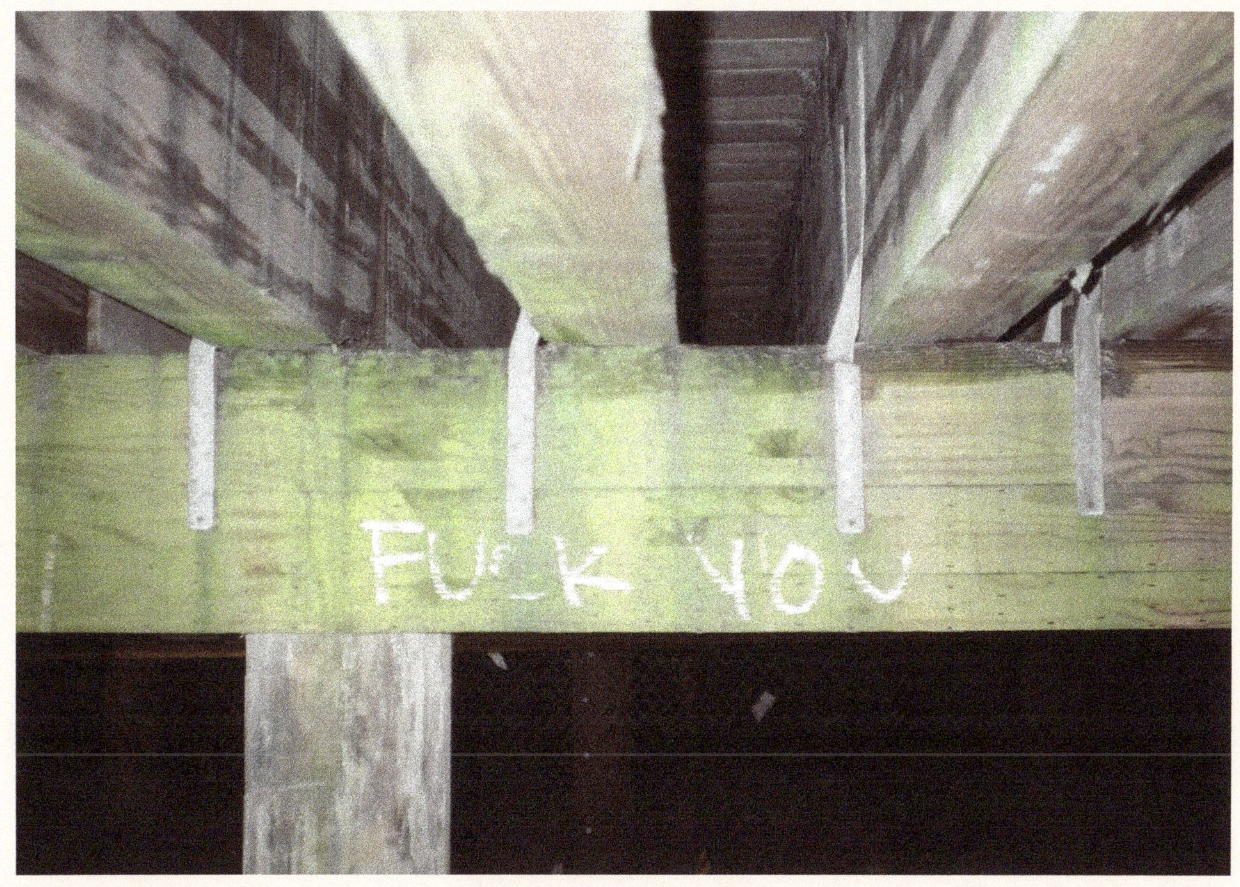

FUCK YOU

REAPING THE BENEFITS OF CHOICE

WORDS WHISP THROUGH THE AIR LIKE THE SMOKE FROM A BLOWN-OUT
CANDLESTICK
SCREAMING AT THE VOICES IN MY MIND WHO HAVE BECOME AMBIVALENT TO
WANDERING EYES
THOSE WHO WATCH FROM A DISTANCE
THOSE WHO STARE TOO LONG
THOSE WHO JUDGE SILENTLY BUT FORCEFULLY
WITH THE FURROW OF A BROW
CONFUSED AT MY IDENTITY
AT MY PRESENTATION OF SELF
BUT I NEVER WISHED TO PLEASE YOU
MY APPEARANCE
MY KINDNESS
MY GRACE
THREATENS YOUR HATE
FOR THE FORCEFUL BLOW OF MY DESIRE FOR CHANGE STRIKES YOU DOWN
SO, ENJOY YOUR MOMENT OF OBSERVATION AND DELIBERATION
THOUGH I ASK...
PLEASE DON'T TOUCH

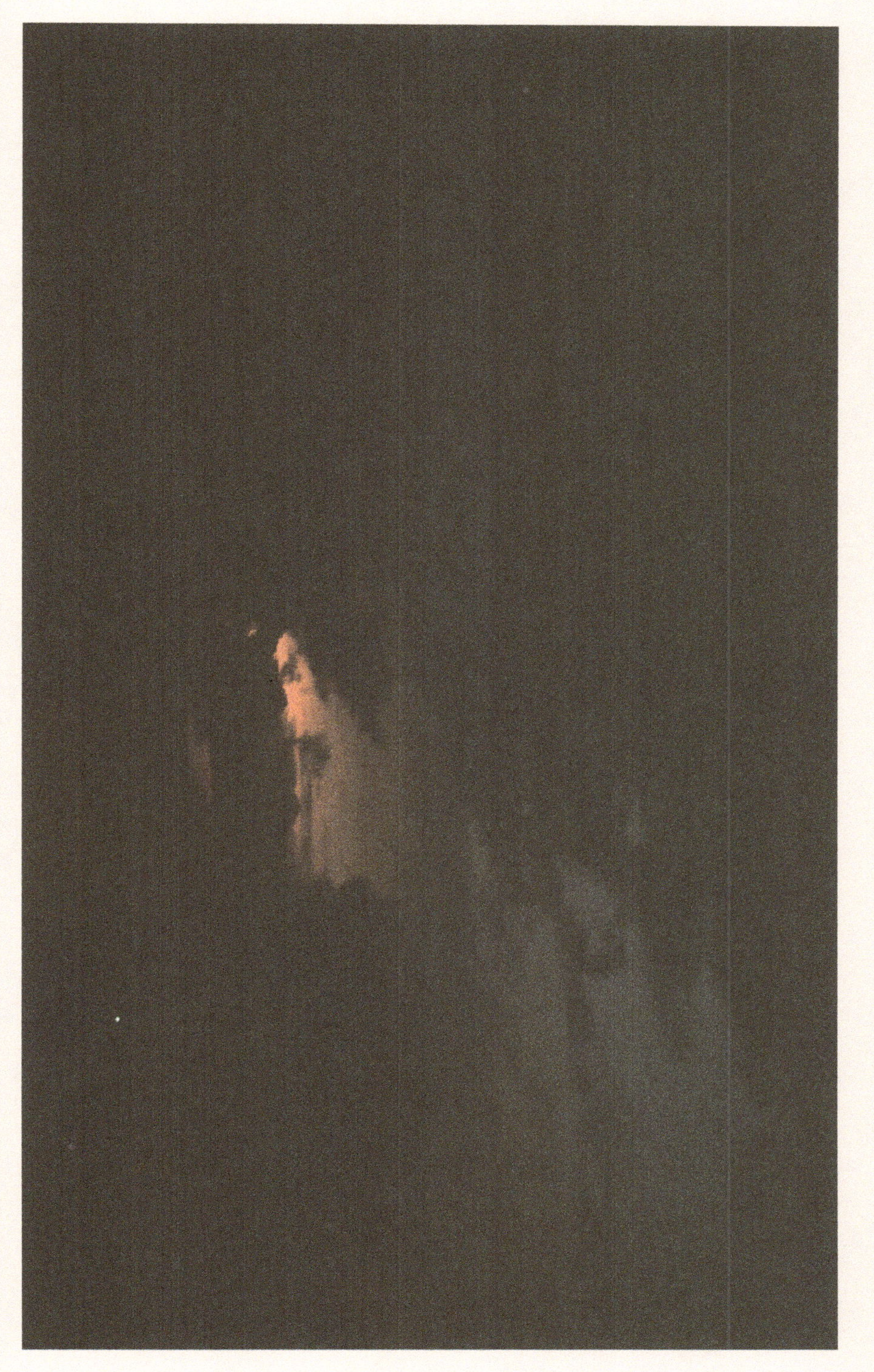

IN THE BUTTERFLY GARDENS

I IMAGINED THE CHARACTER OF YOU IN THE MEADOWS OF WESTERN
PENNSYLVANIA
SOMEWHERE
IN OUR AWFUL REALITY
I KNEW I WOULD NEVER GO TO FIND YOU
SEARCHING FOR MY SAN JOSE IN A BUTTERFLY GARDEN
PICKING UP EVERY STONE, LOOKING
PEERING BEHIND EVERY SPRUCE, LOOKING
WADING THROUGH OPEN WATER, LOOKING

I SAW NOTHING BUT MY DISHEVELED REFLECTION IN THE TAINTED WATERS
OF THE STREAM
STARING BACK WITH HALF-SHUT EYES AND ABRASIVE SKIN
WHO HAD I BECOME IN MY SEARCH FOR YOU?
WHAT DID I LOSE TRYING TO FIND A PIECE OF A STORYLINE YOU
COULDN'T WRITE?

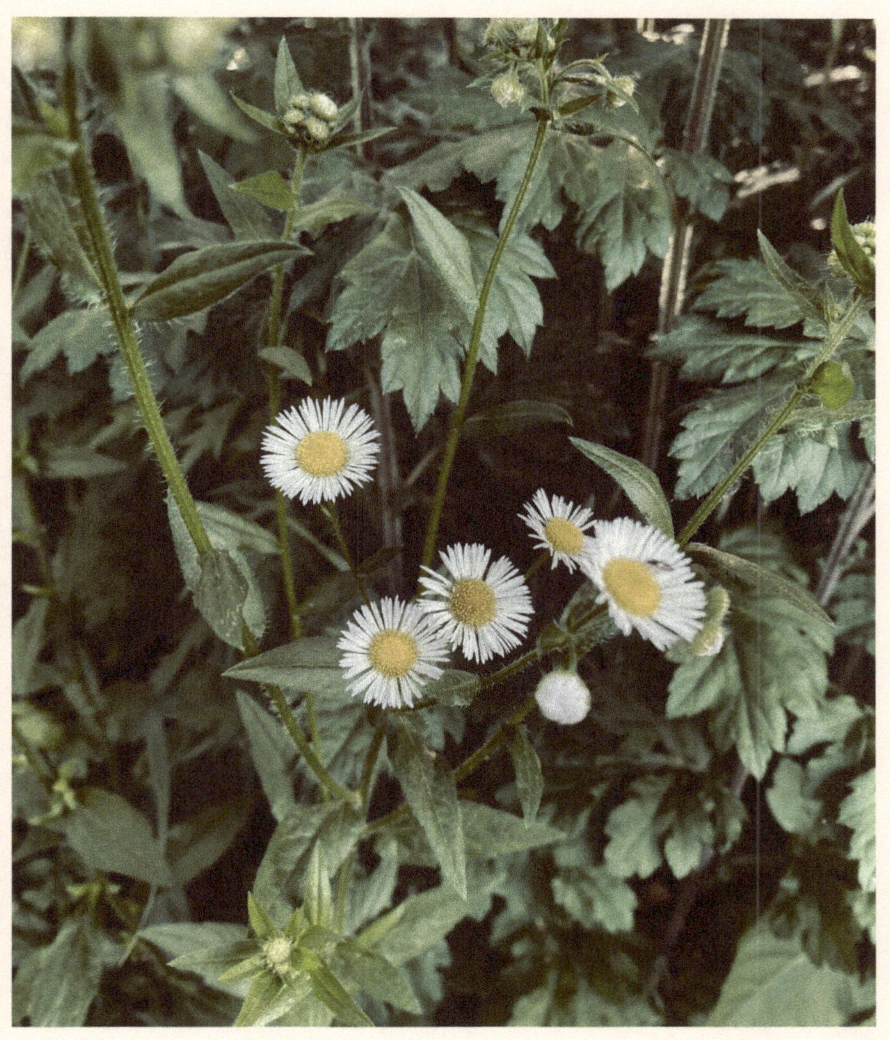

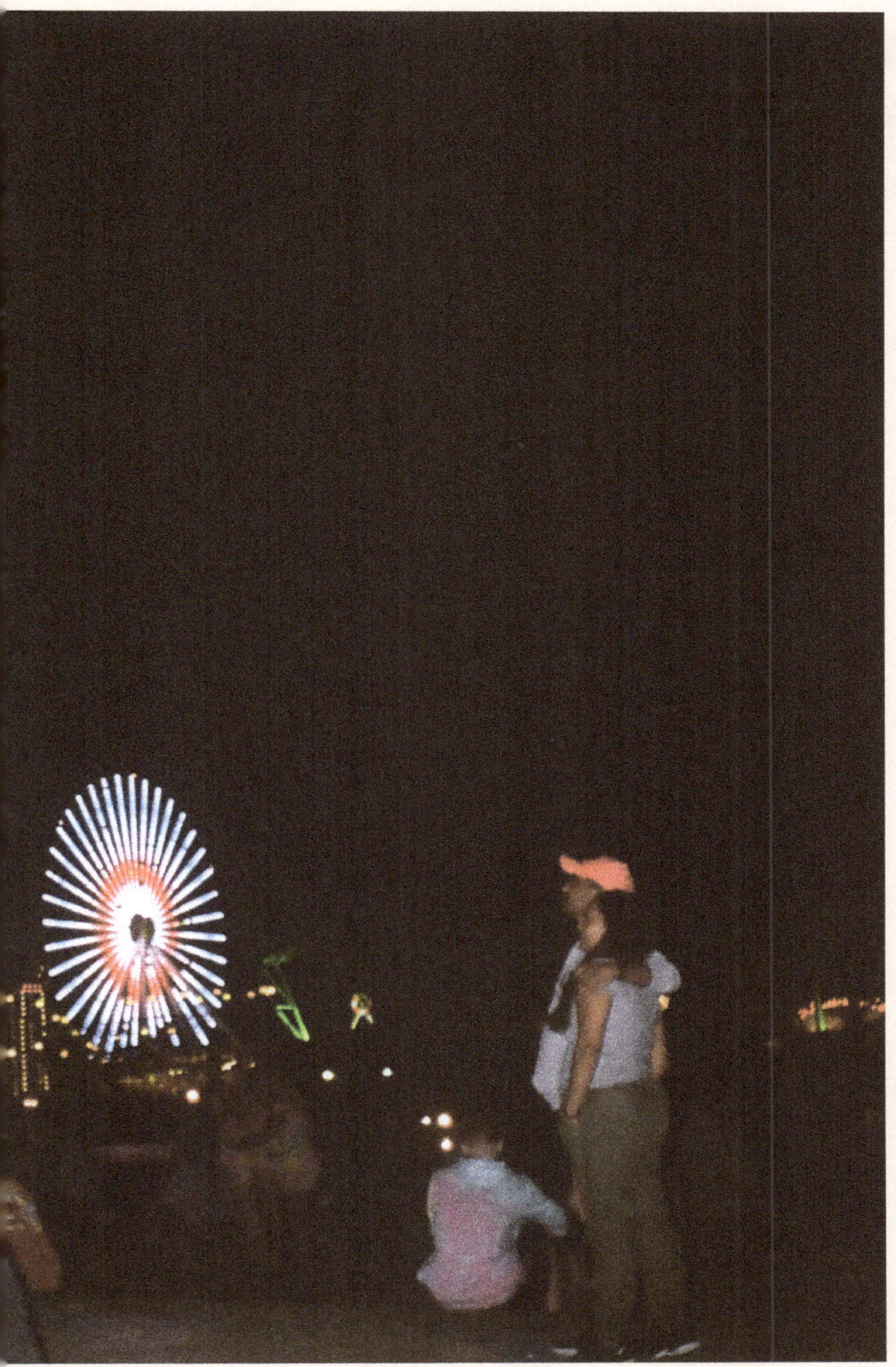

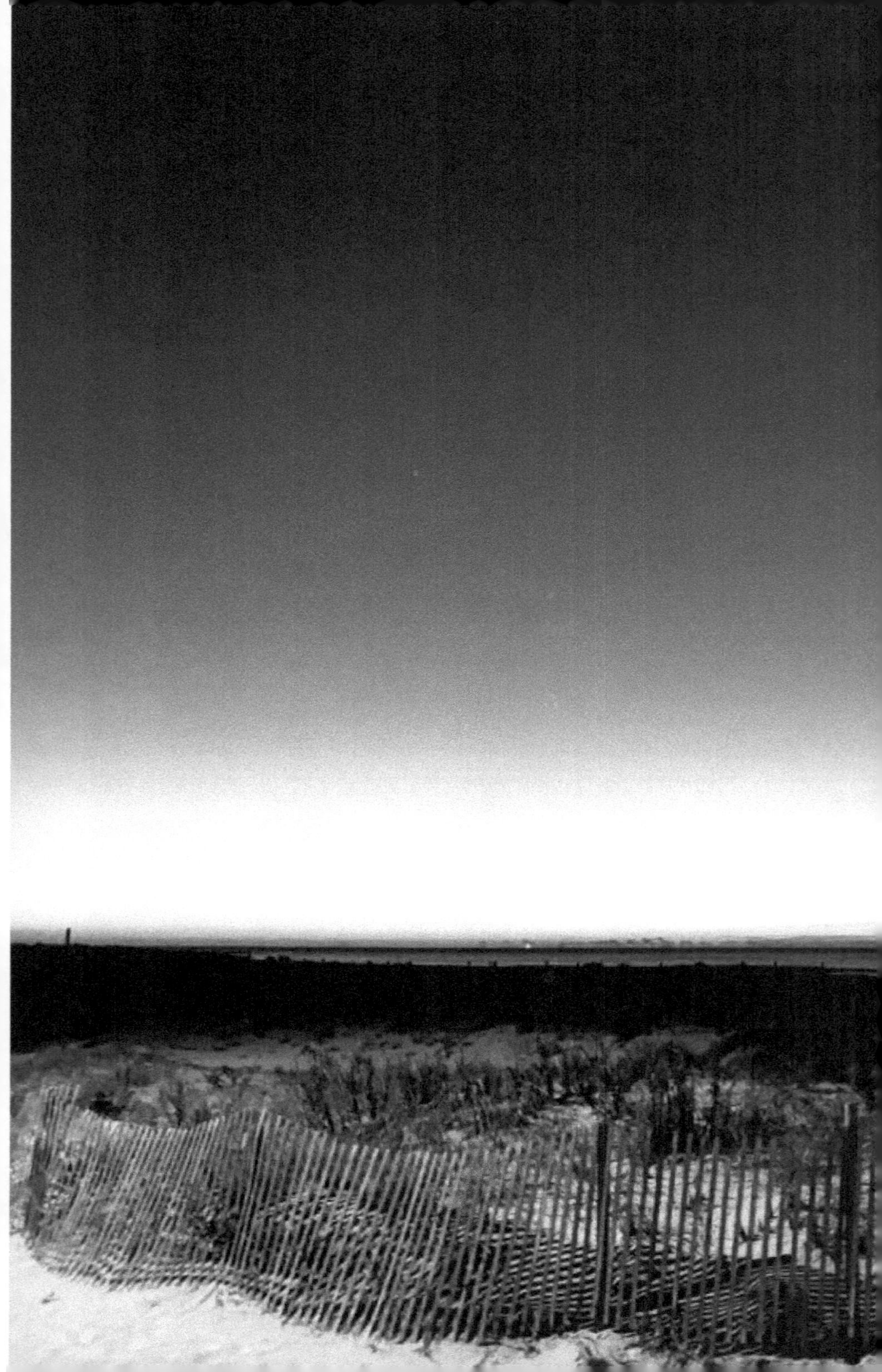

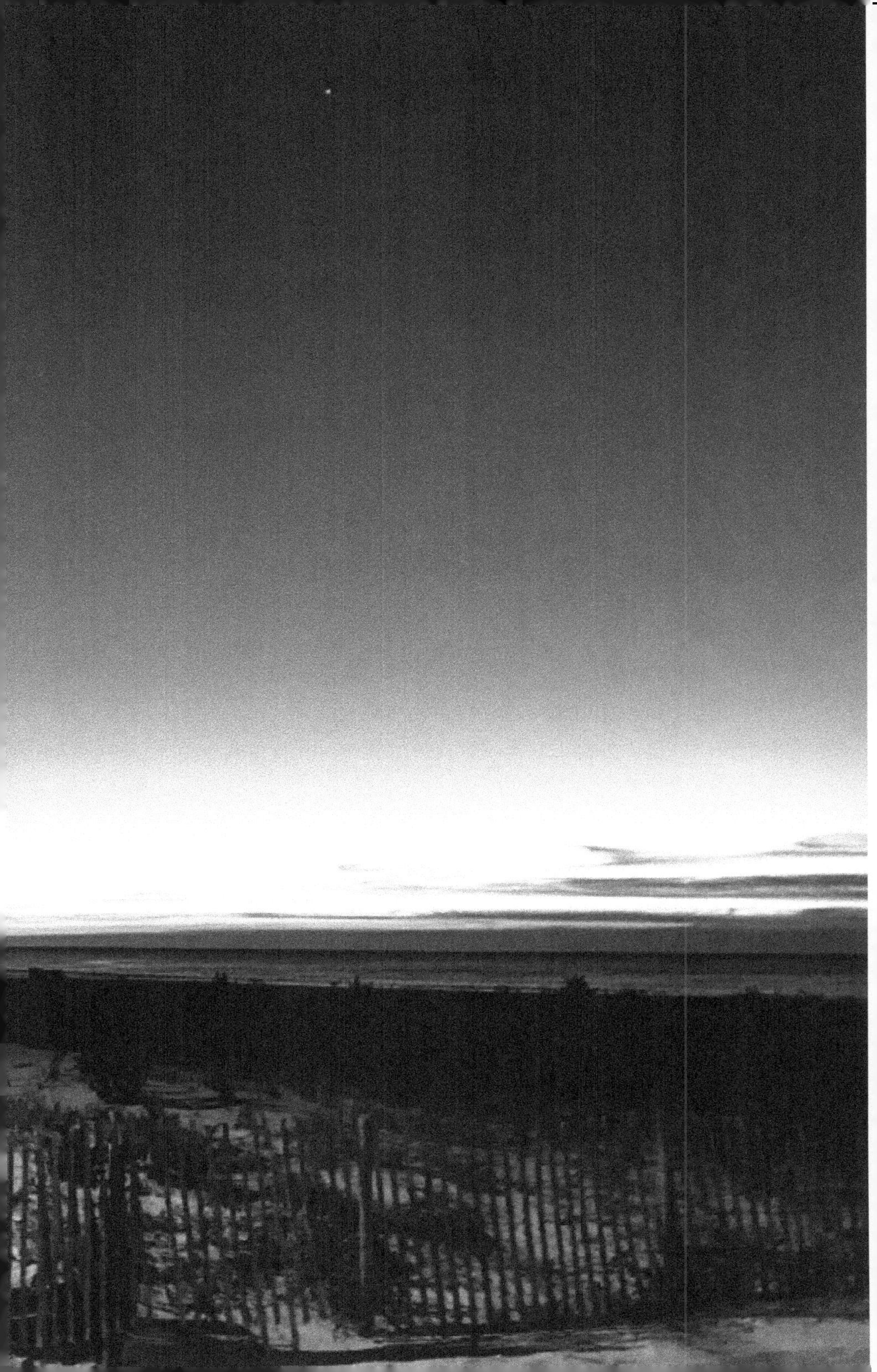

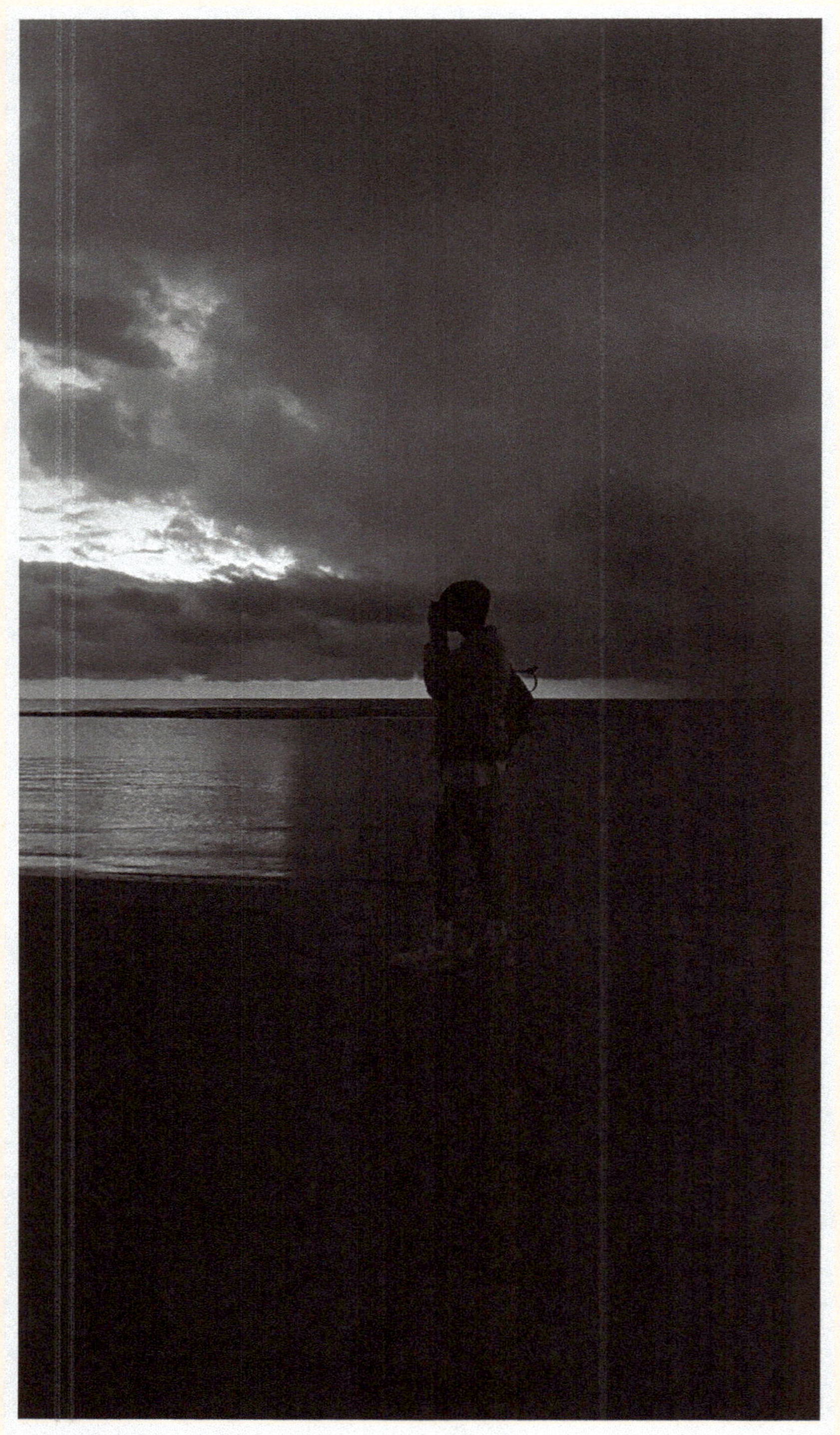

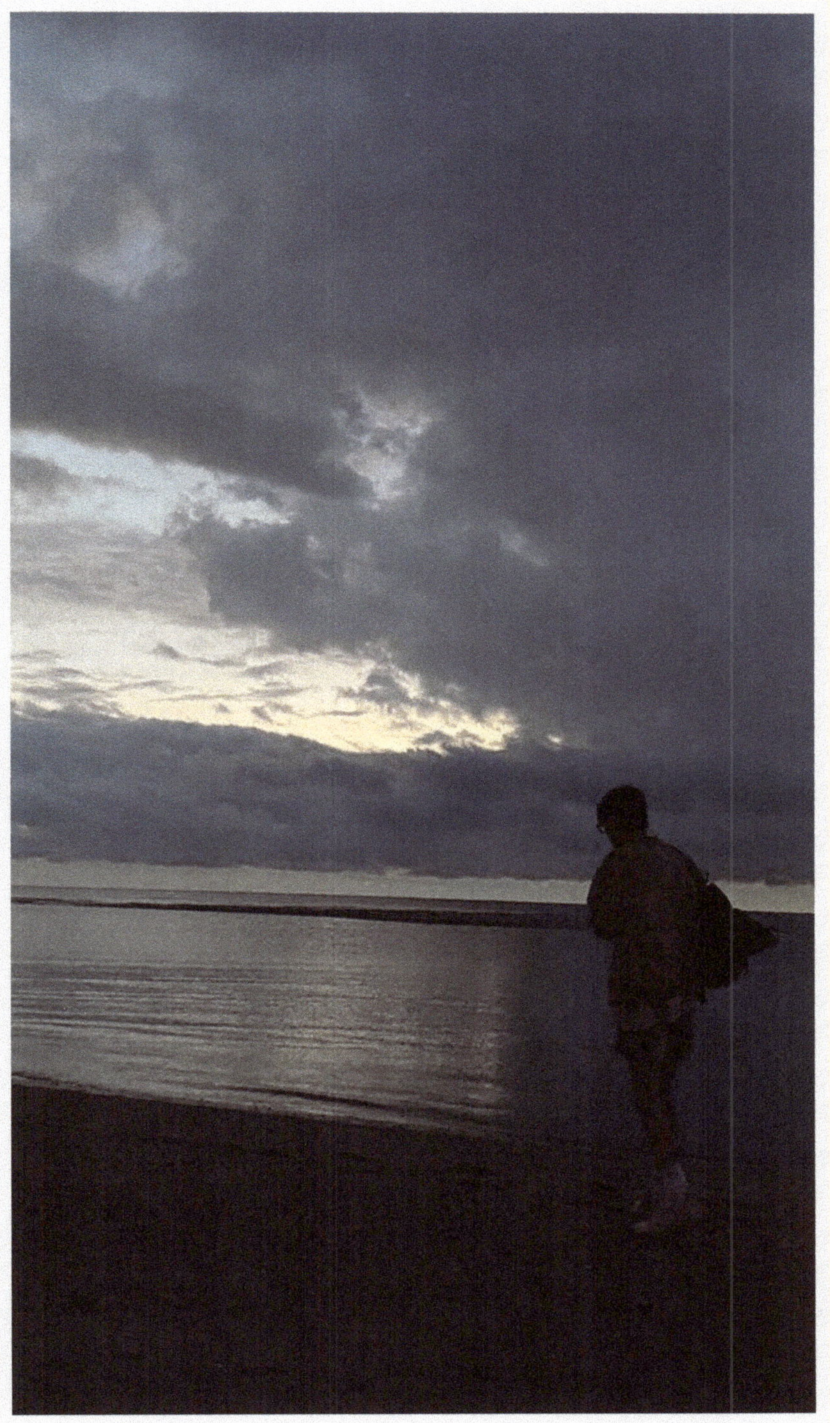

THE DOLL MAKER

You always liked the camera
And I admired that
A flash of light
Quiet but violent
Filling the void between us
Short but dense
Because I watched you fall
Gradually
But with force
From the hand of a man
Who told you he was your maker
Painted your eyes with titanium white
Crafted your dress from the finest of silks
Carved your skin from the bark of cherry
All to watch you break
A tantalizing game of your destruction
One you never wished to play
One you never dared to speak of
Even to me

Until the day
You made contact with the concrete
Cold and unforgiving
A dead end to a game you became a victim of
A game you never wished to play

I picked up your broken pieces
And patched you together
To the best of my ability
And I forever will
So if you fall once more...

Fall onto me.

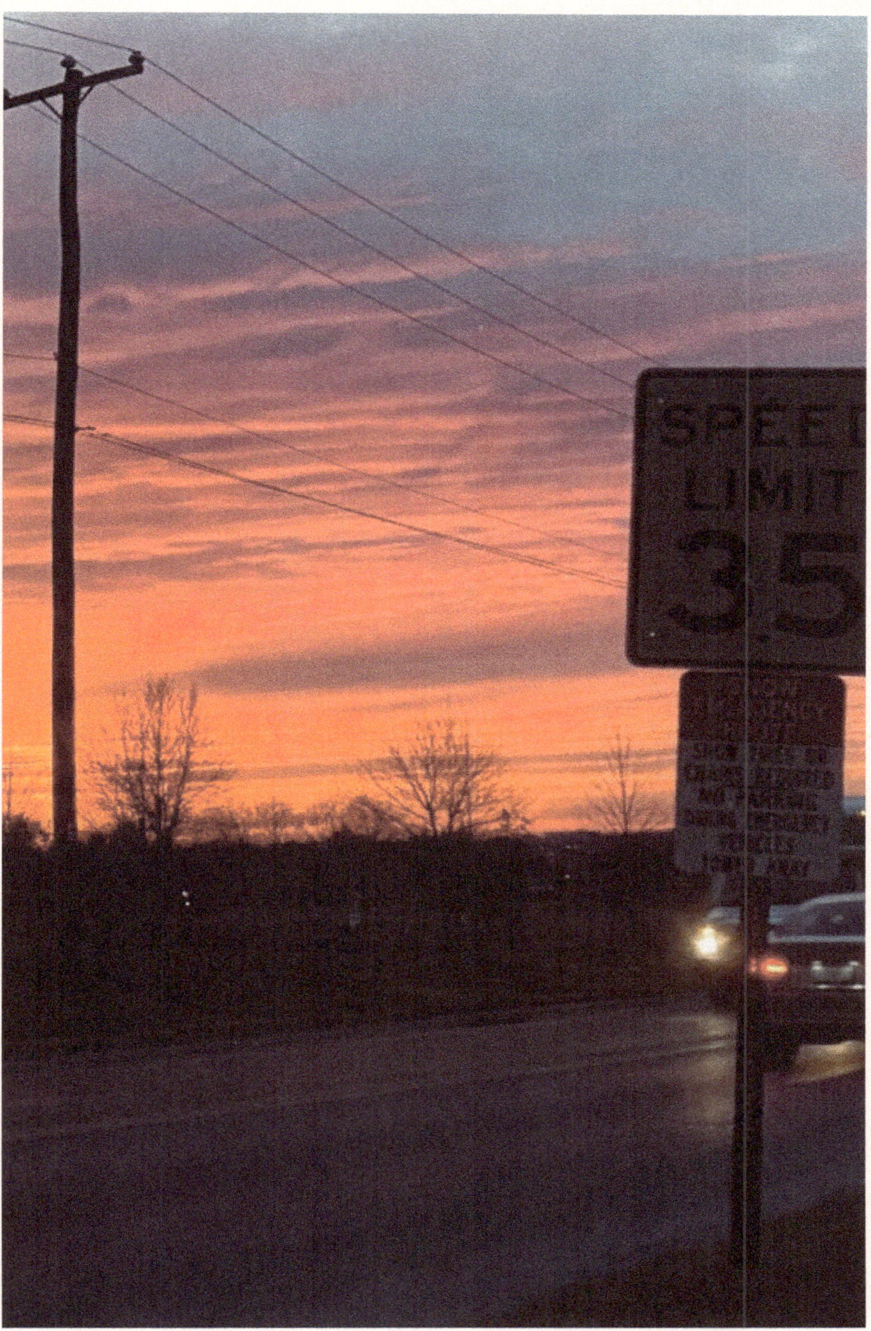

SPEED
LIMIT
35

THE PLATTE RIVER

I never believed I could miss you
Until my world crumbled
Piece by piece
And you were the only place I could go
To find the origins of me

The grasslands were silent
And so was I
Watching the wind grasp the labyrinth of fields that laid before
me
Rustling
Shaking
Chaotic beauty
The sky was a watercolor
Hues of:
Orange
Pink
Yellow
Pleaded for my attention

The Earth before me drifted
Pulsated
Came to life
So I sat unfazed by the world's need for an audience
But when I saw you
I ran to you
Until I realized you were nothing but a fragment of a
broken mind
So I coiled up into a ball
Tears falling
Filling up the Platte
Just About 20 miles past timbuktu
The reflection I saw in the waters was one of horror
Unrecognizable…
I dove in.

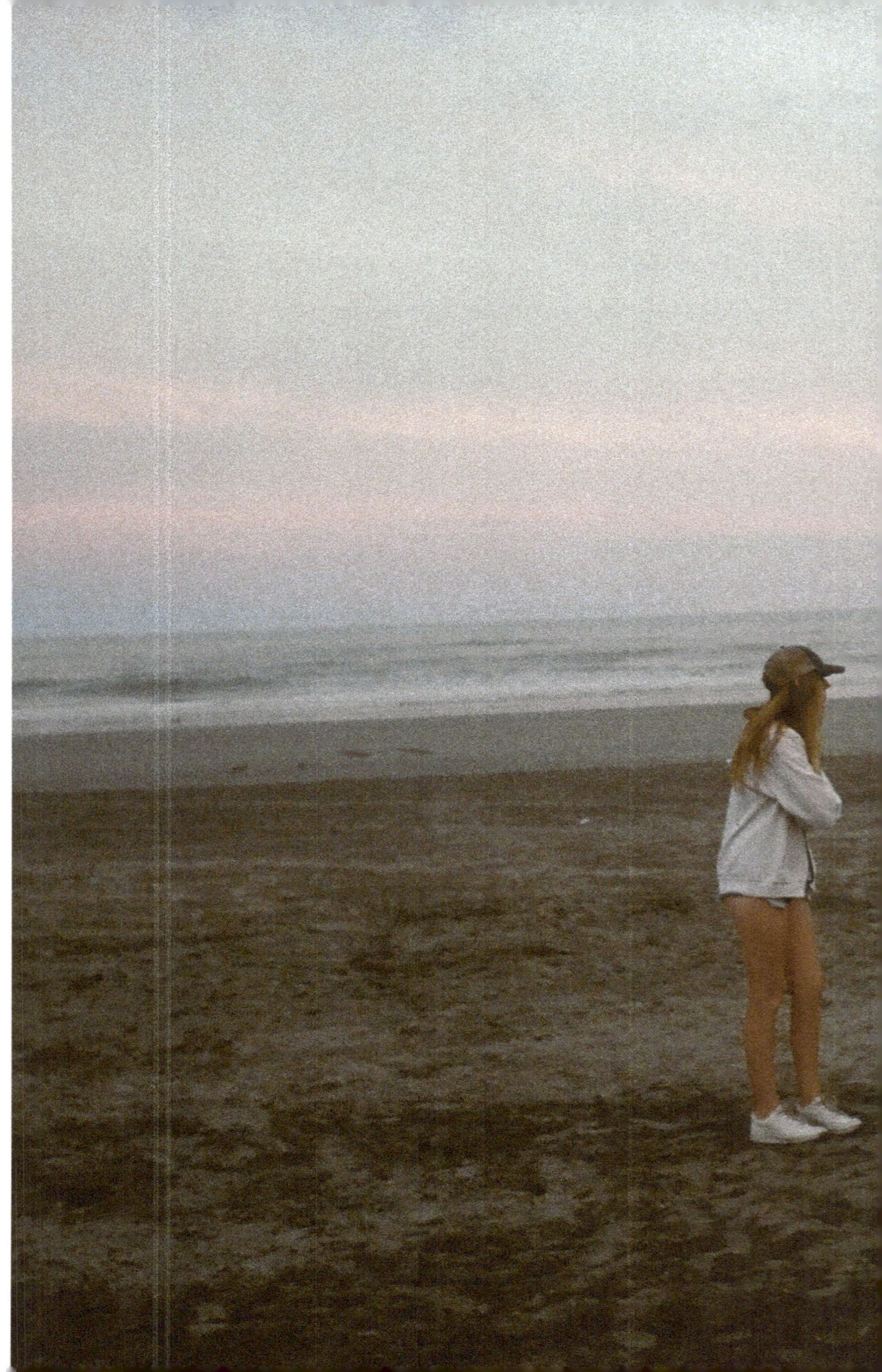

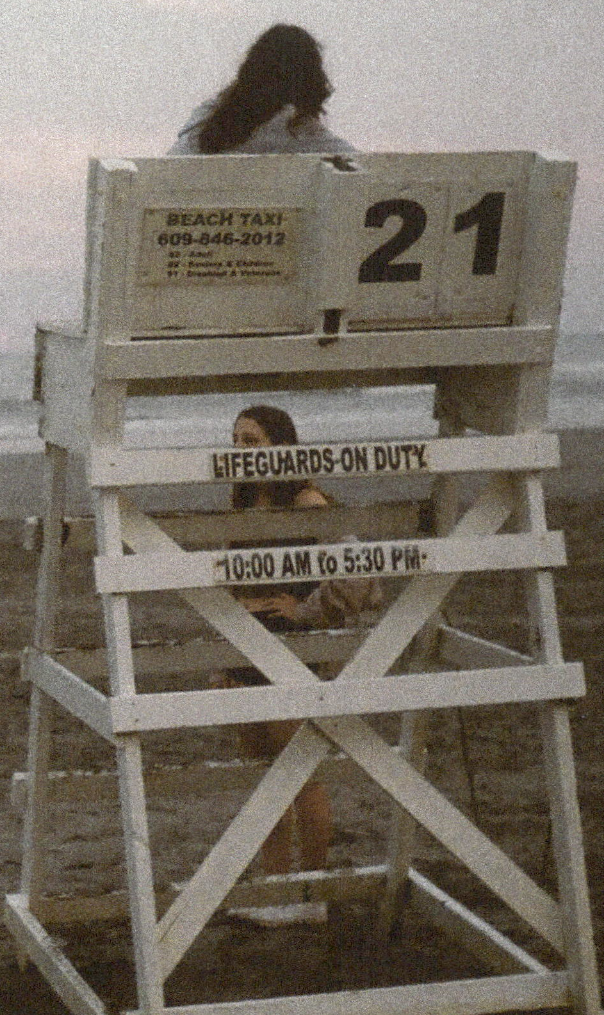

BEACH TAXI
609-846-2012
21
LIFEGUARDS ON DUTY
10:00 AM to 5:30 PM

THE RAINBOW I NEVER WAS

I COULD BE ANYTHING
EVERY COLOR OF THE RAINBOW
EVERY SHADE OF BLUE IN THE SEA
ANYTHING TO KEEP YOU HERE NEXT TO ME
BUT YOU LEFT SO QUICKLY
DIDN'T EVEN SAY GOODBYE
AND NOW ALL I CAN DO IS ASK MYSELF WHY?

WHY WAS I INFATUATED WITH YOUR EXISTENCE?
FOR WHAT DO YOU OFFER THAT I DON'T ALREADY HAVE
CONFUSION?
FRUSTRATION?
DISAPPOINTMENT?
THE FRUITS OF YOUR LABOR AND MY ANGER
MAYBE IT'S BEST IF I REJECT IT ALL
PRETEND IT WAS A FANTASY
A FALSE REALITY
FOR OUR STORY COULD ONLY EVER EXIST IN A DRIFTING MIND

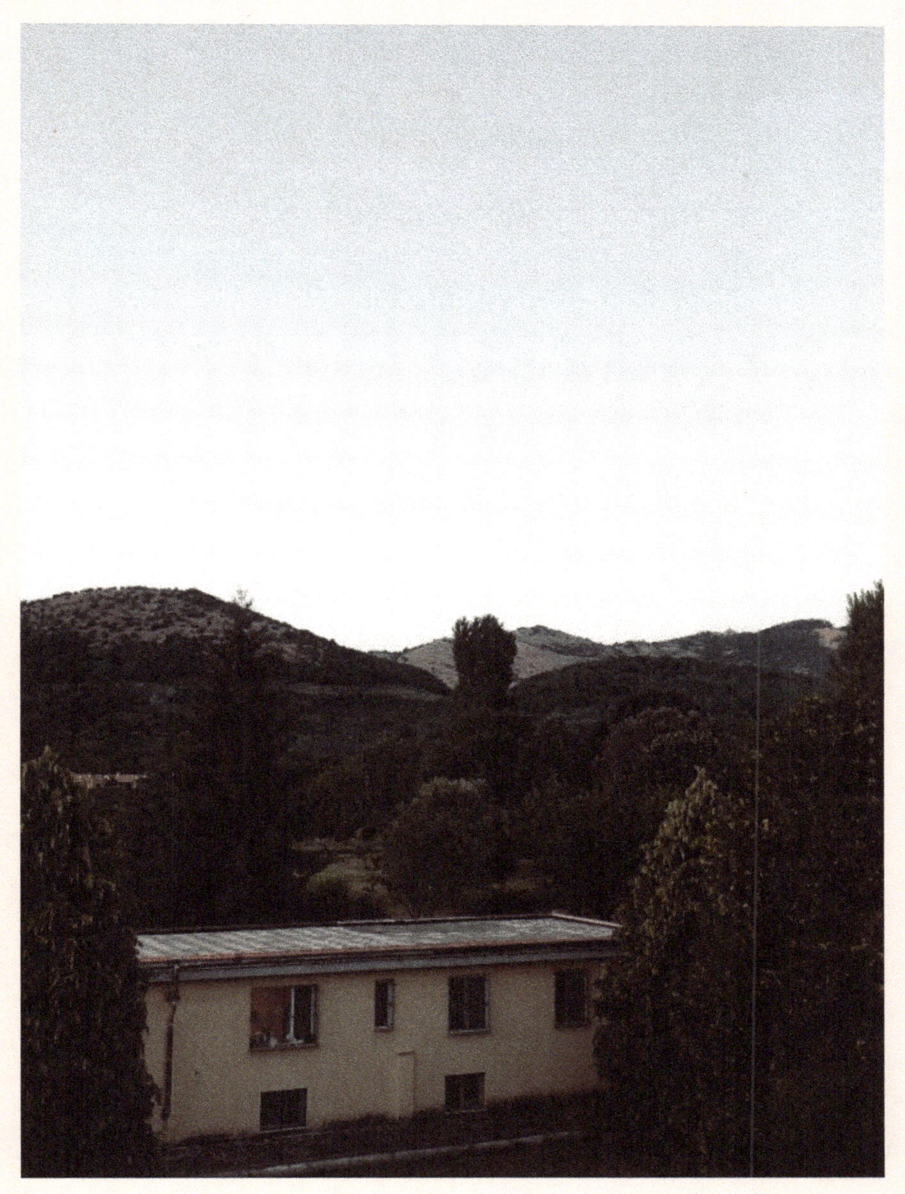

SILENCE IN DECEMBER

Two years of growth
But I never heard a thing
December arrived and I wished upon your star
Regretting such action in coming days
But there was silence upon spring's arrival
Upon the blossoming of myself
Into beautiful pastels
And you wished nothing of such color
How could I expect you to?
And when our timeline turned I wished upon the December Star once more
Your acknowledgment of such being the validation I craved
But when the roses sang
And when the tall grasses danced
I heard nothing but silence
Angering silence
Envy
Frustration
Rage
Filling the void of sound
Chaos erupts in the stillness of nothing

Silence reveled in her mystery
In her unknown facets of self
And I hated her
Until she removed her dressings
Revealing her secrets of an immortal existence
That her presence was minute on the vastness of sound
For one may open a window and harmonize with the singing
trapeze walkers of the natural world
Who provide peace in their rejection of silence
So.
By living in sound.
I search for peace with you.

AT THE DRIVE THRU

You called out to me
But when I reached for you there was nothing there
An intense dream
A mirage in the mind
Is what you slowly became
As I swallowed the pill that was understanding your mind had changed
But it hurts so much
Because I can't find it in me to blame you

The portrait below me
The reflection before me
You next to me
By the way
I had always thought you were cute too
Just never had it in me to confess
And now I'm painted blue

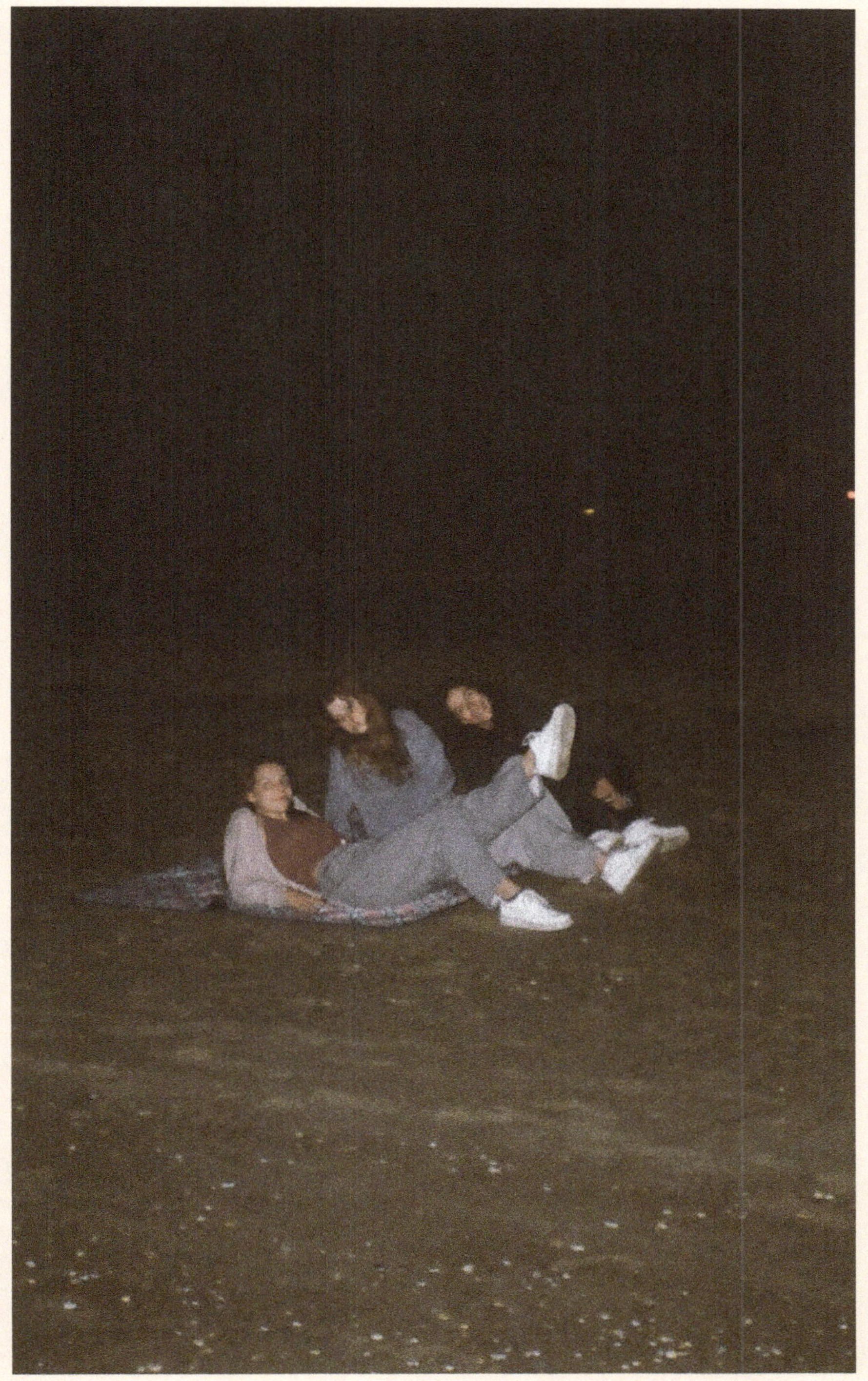

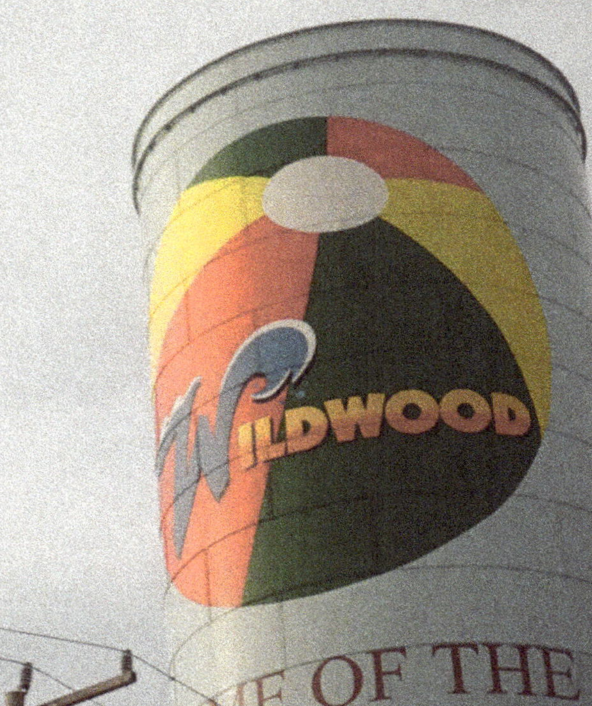
Wildwood
OME OF THE
WARRIORS

I saw you along 422
Somewhere deep in an intrusive thought
Pacing the pavement as I sang "our" song
Thunder crashing
Lightning striking
Chaos tearing the world at its seams
You sat and waited
Seemed almost afraid
So I yelled to you out the passenger side window
Pleading for some sort of rescue story
You got in
Hesitantly
Shut the door
And sat Silently
I couldn't notice anything but the contours of your face
The cars around us became lost from my gaze
A blur of light and color
Until it was only you and I
Your words rolled off the tongue
"I'm on fire"
So I lit my match
Just as you had
And burned the canvas blank once again

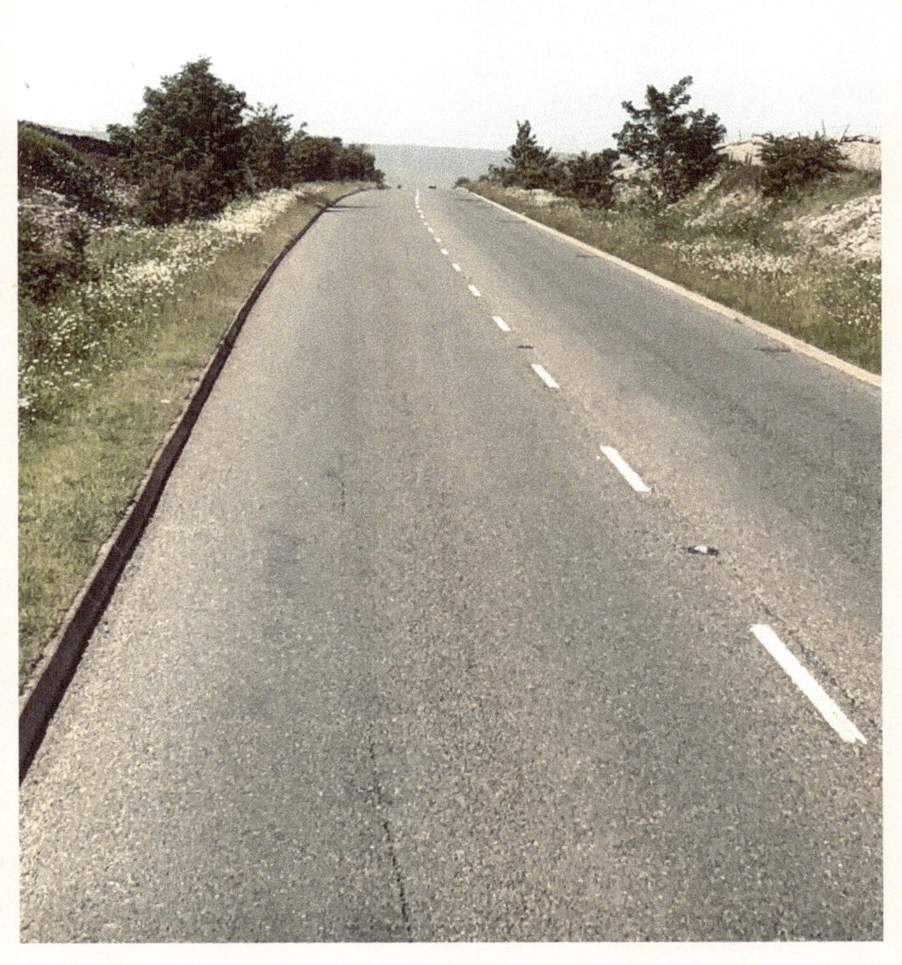

THE GALLERY

I could never trust you
Because you weren't who I designed in my mind
The man I made up
The version of you I created for my own comfort
A selfish act
And now I despise you
And I never want to see the letters
Or hear the vowels of your name spoken off the tongue
For the pain of infinite waiting
And sustained failure
Has become too much to bear
But the vibrancy of the artwork I created for you
Of you
Lives within the walls of my mind
And the pages of this book
That maybe one day you will buy off of the shelf
Unaware of your presence among the print
And that is all I could ever want…

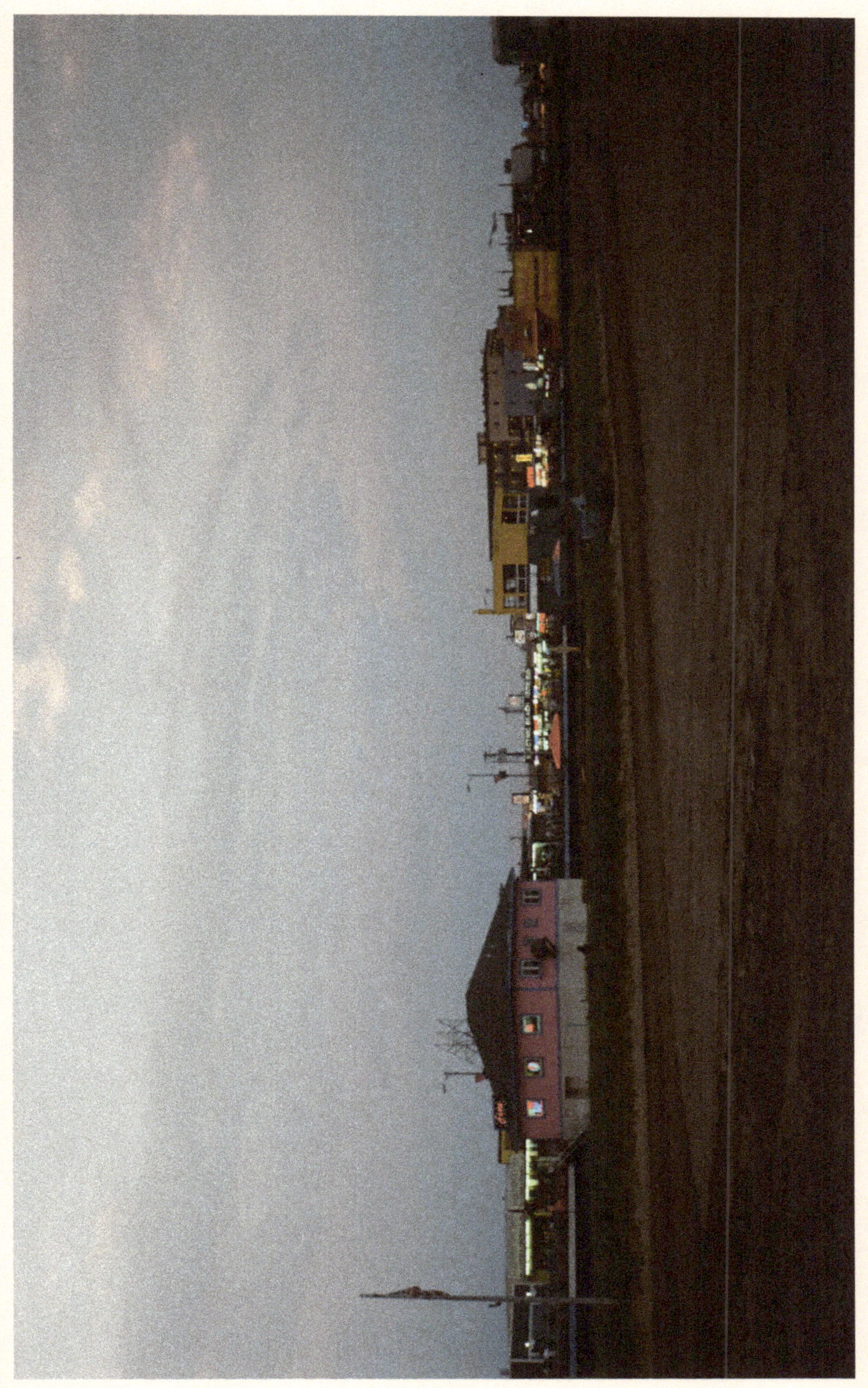

CALLS FROM BEHIND THE GLASS PANES

I live trapped
Suffocated by closed doors
Surrounded by the bars of my metaphorical cage that restrains my
identity
But I paint the walls in ever color of the rainbow
And I make every effort to escape
Break free from my own entrapment
Or society's entrapment?
Maybe both

Here and there light breaks through
Revealing the beauty born of my creative asphyxiation
Giving me hope for potential freedom
Freedom that calls to me late at night
Keeping me up
Tossing
Turning
The urge to be everything
To feel everything
To see everything
To be a part of something

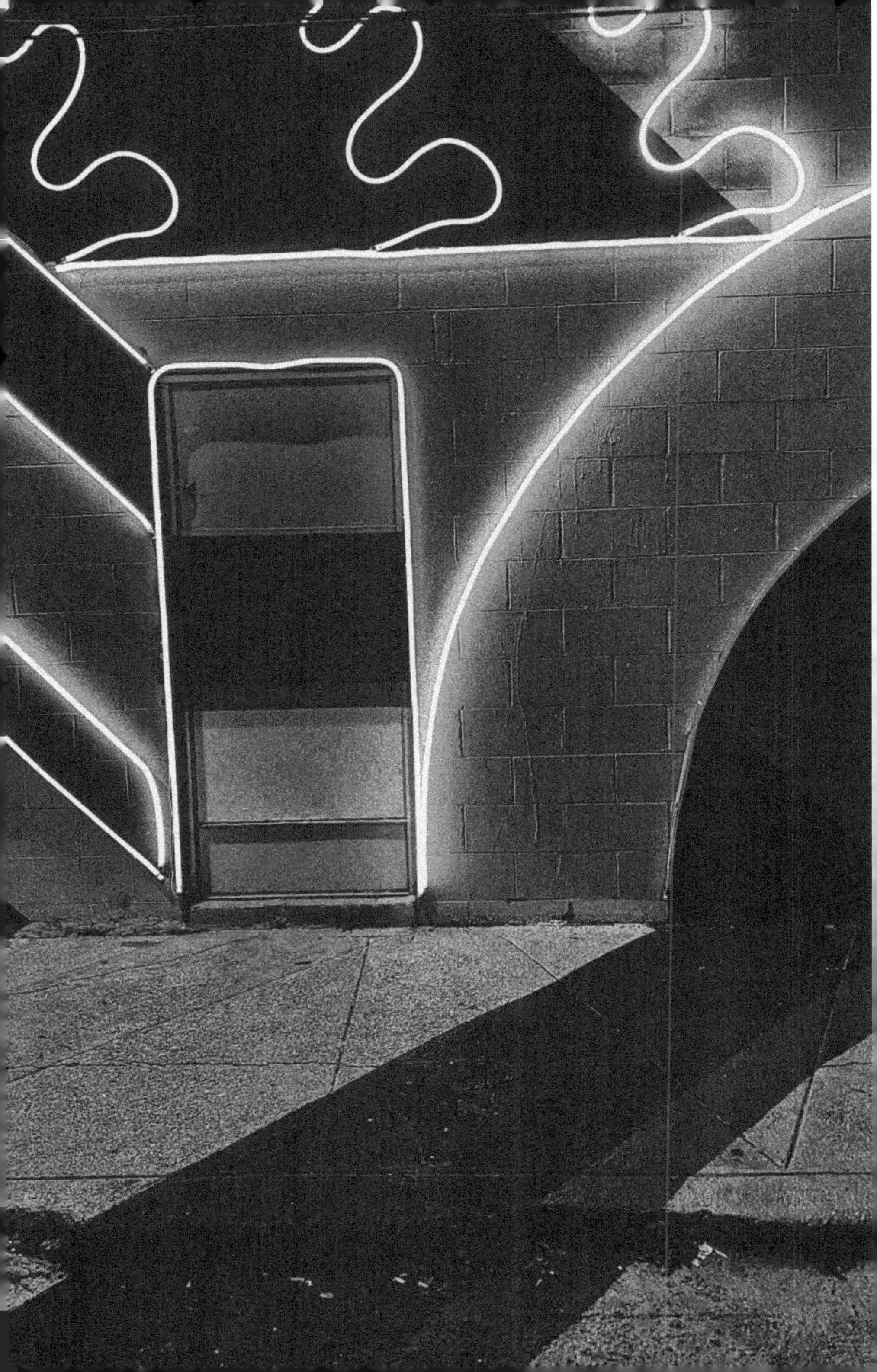

FIRES IN THE PALACE GARDENS

The ease of my enragement
The anger to shatter the golden framed, glistening mirrors of Versailles
Where I imagined we sat in the gardens
Surrounded by flames and fleeing tourists
But I couldn't find the energy to care
And neither did you
So we watched silently
As beauty burned
And chaos erupted

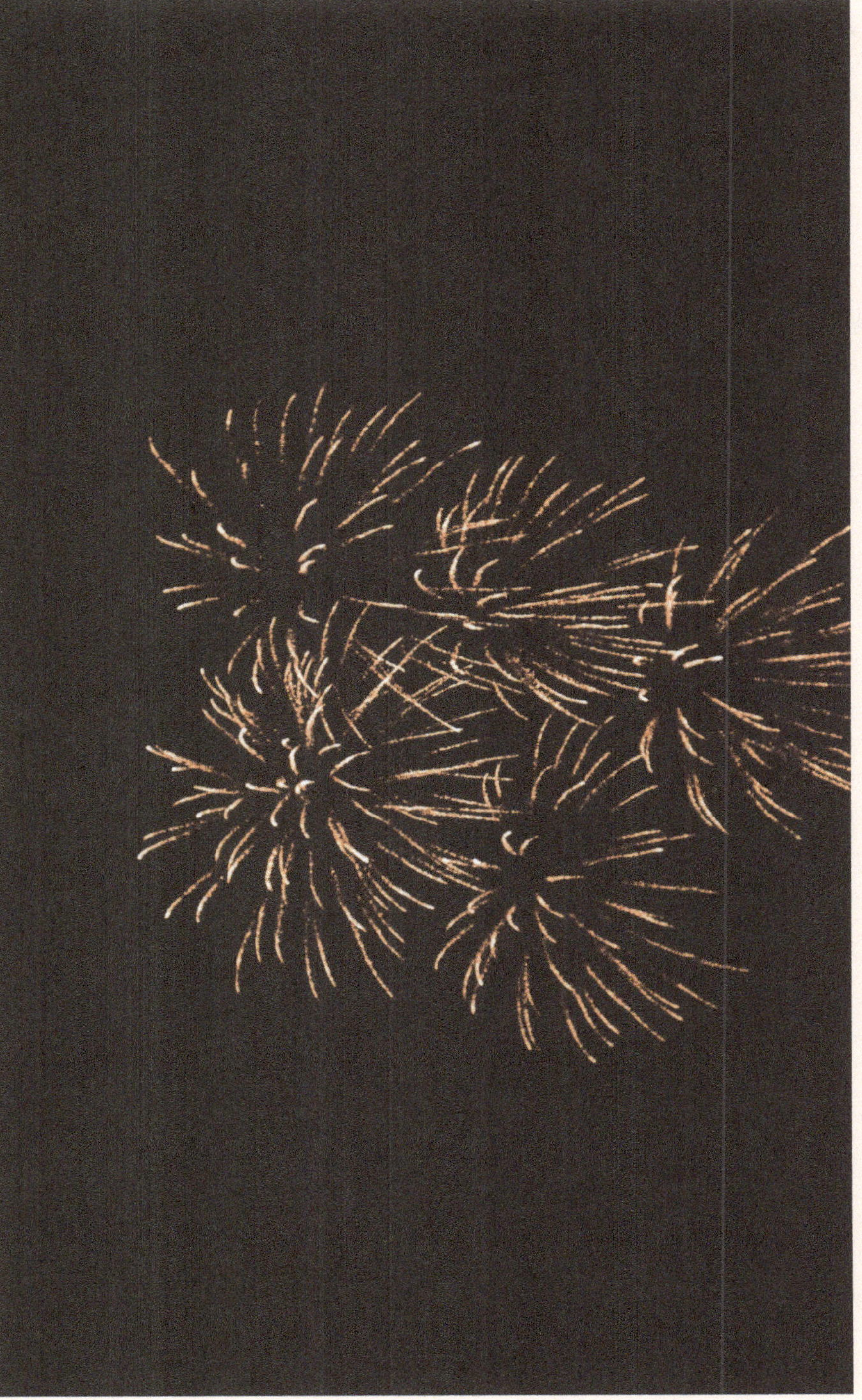

THE GARDEN GATE

Bianca was red
Sydney was blue
Sarah was green

Elena was purple
Bridget was orange
Simone was pink

Every color of the rainbow
I was made to think

They wandered the paths of the gardens
Where many storylines…
Converged
Diverged
The birthplace and graveyard of the moments of my experience
They cut the roses
They polished the marble fountains
They watered the dying citrus trees
But most importantly
The gardens were stripped of their gold leaf
So i would never lose sight of the greenery
Of the color
Of the beauty
That grew gradually with time
Inside of me
Inside all of them
So I write a thank you to you now
And hope you understand my gratitude
When I say

My gardens will always be a home to you.

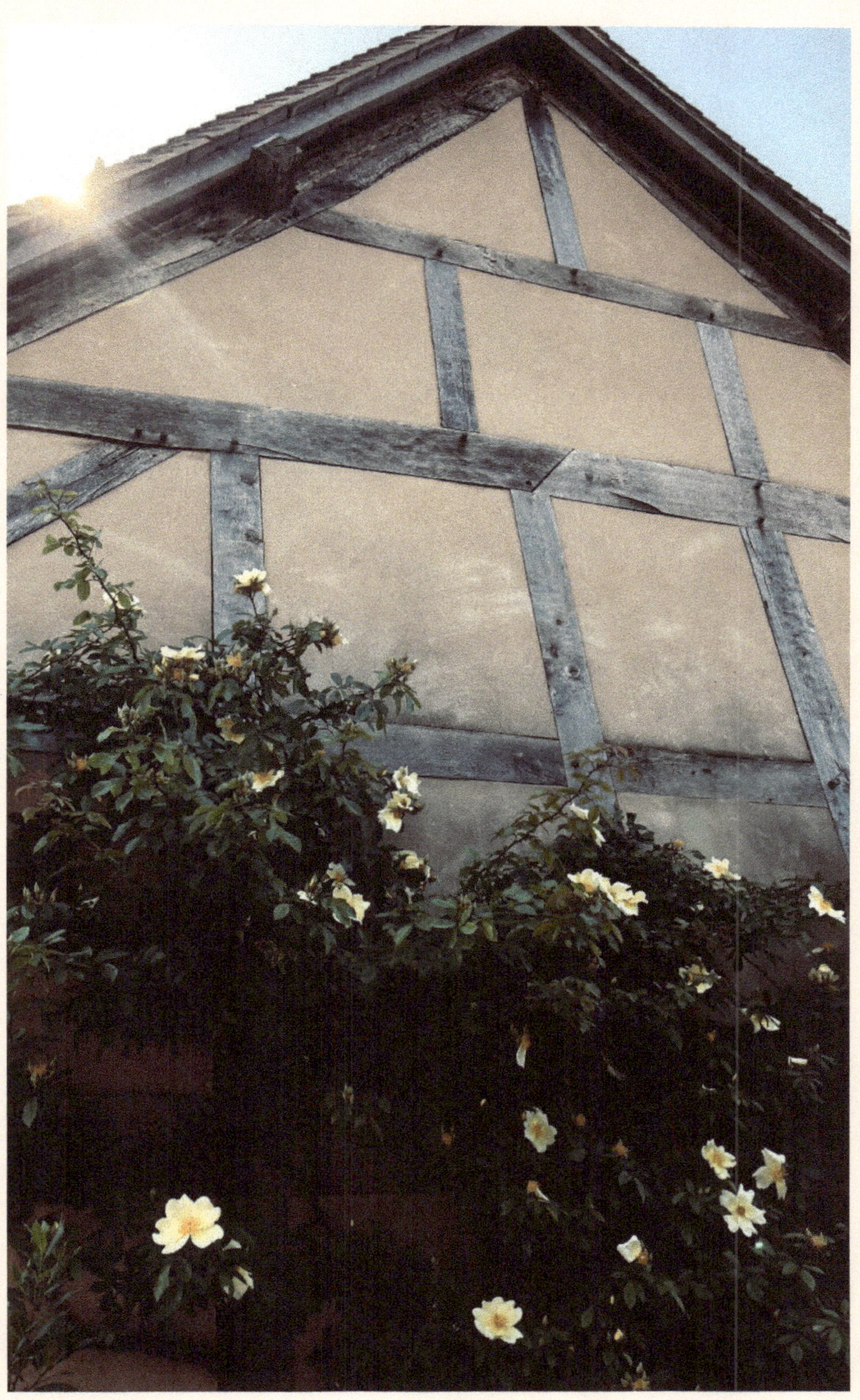

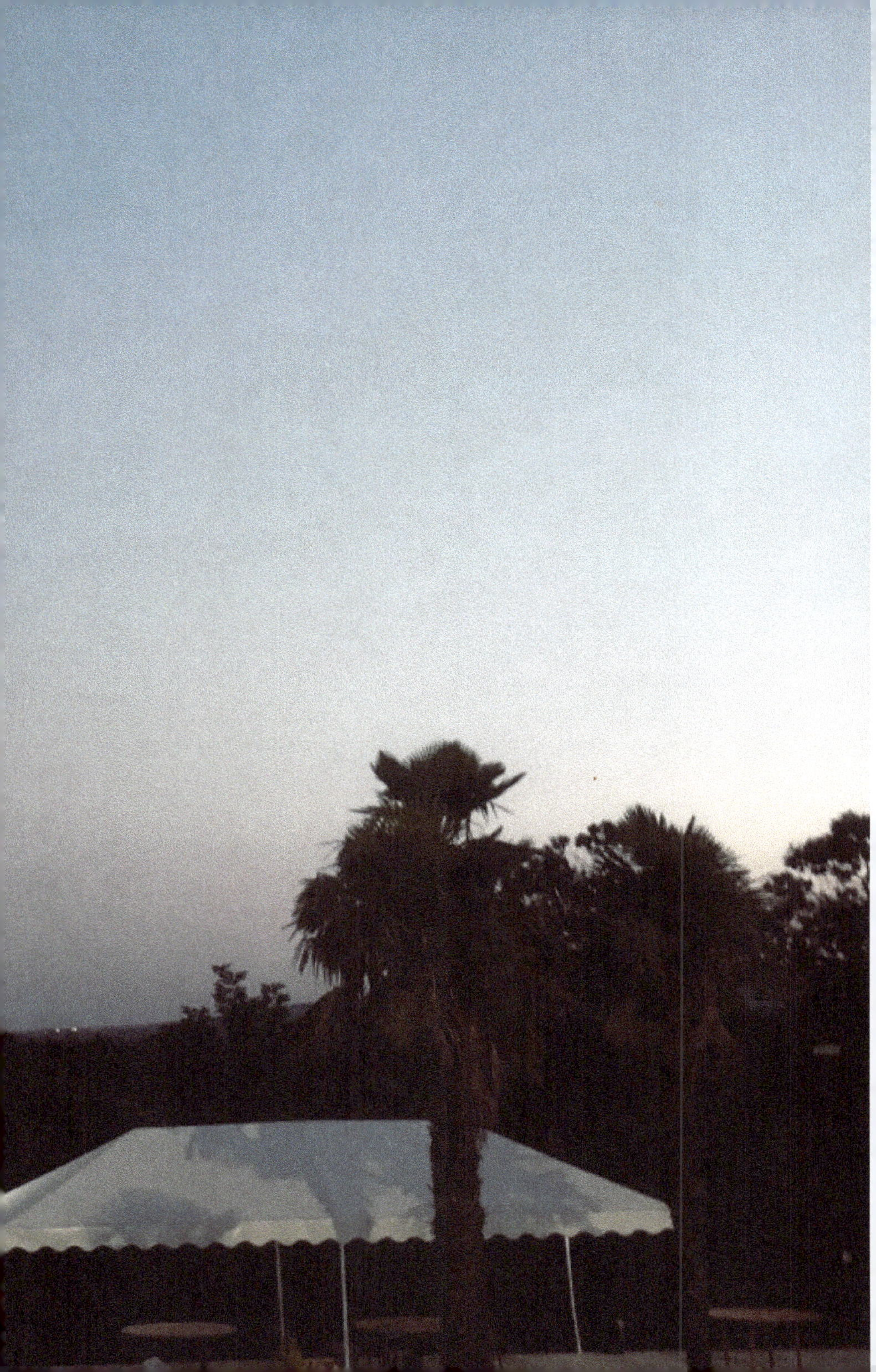

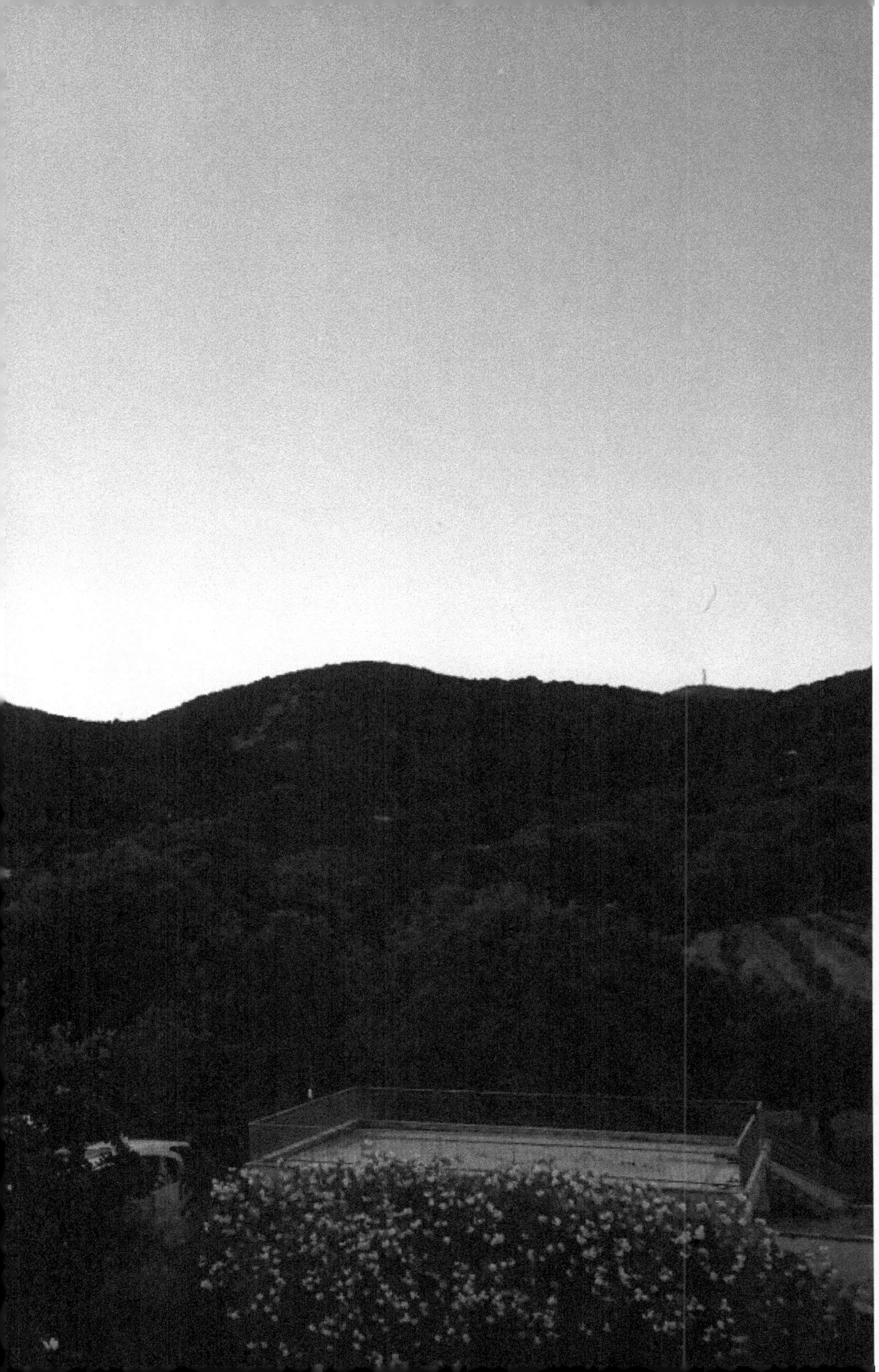

"notes for a poet"

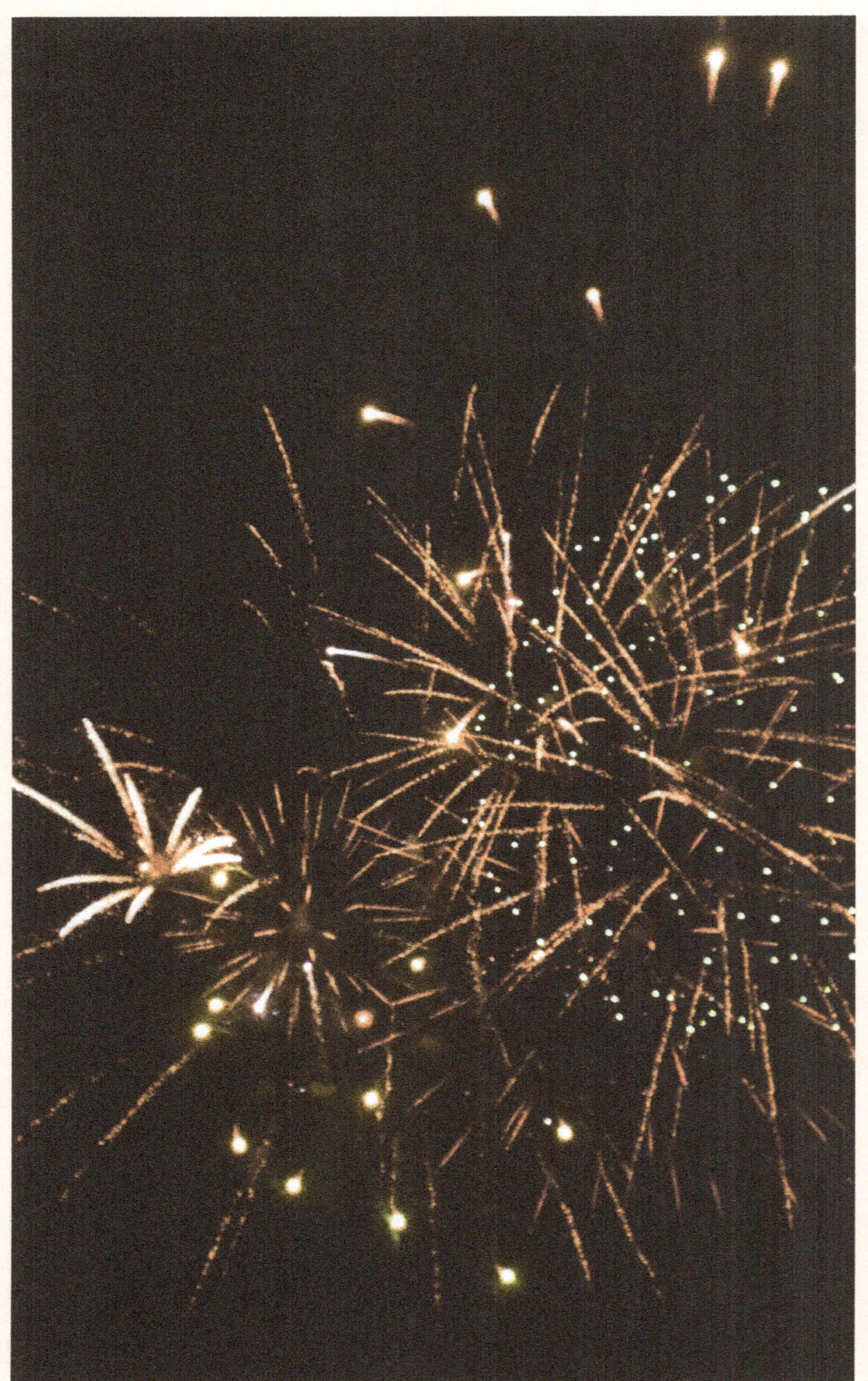

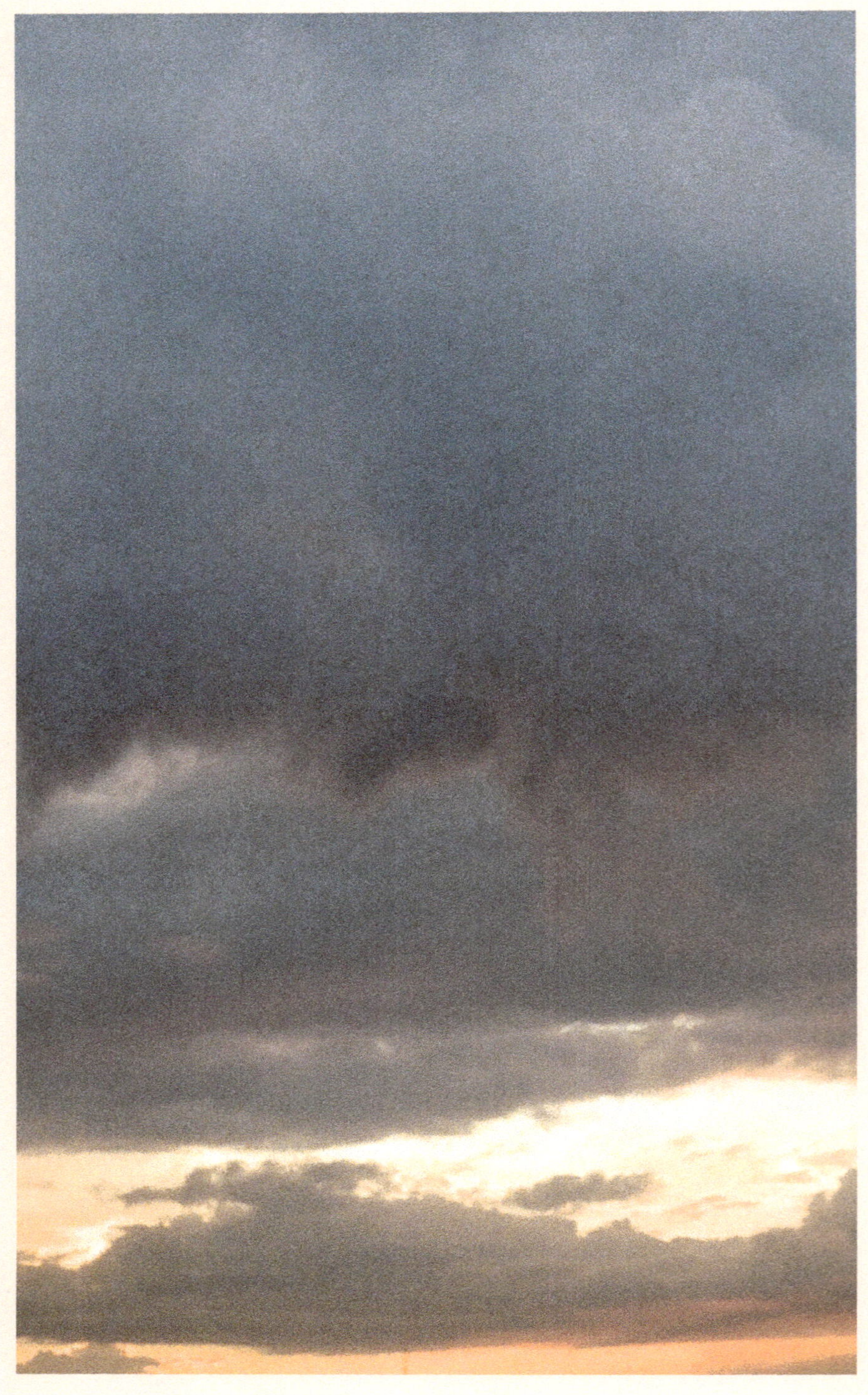

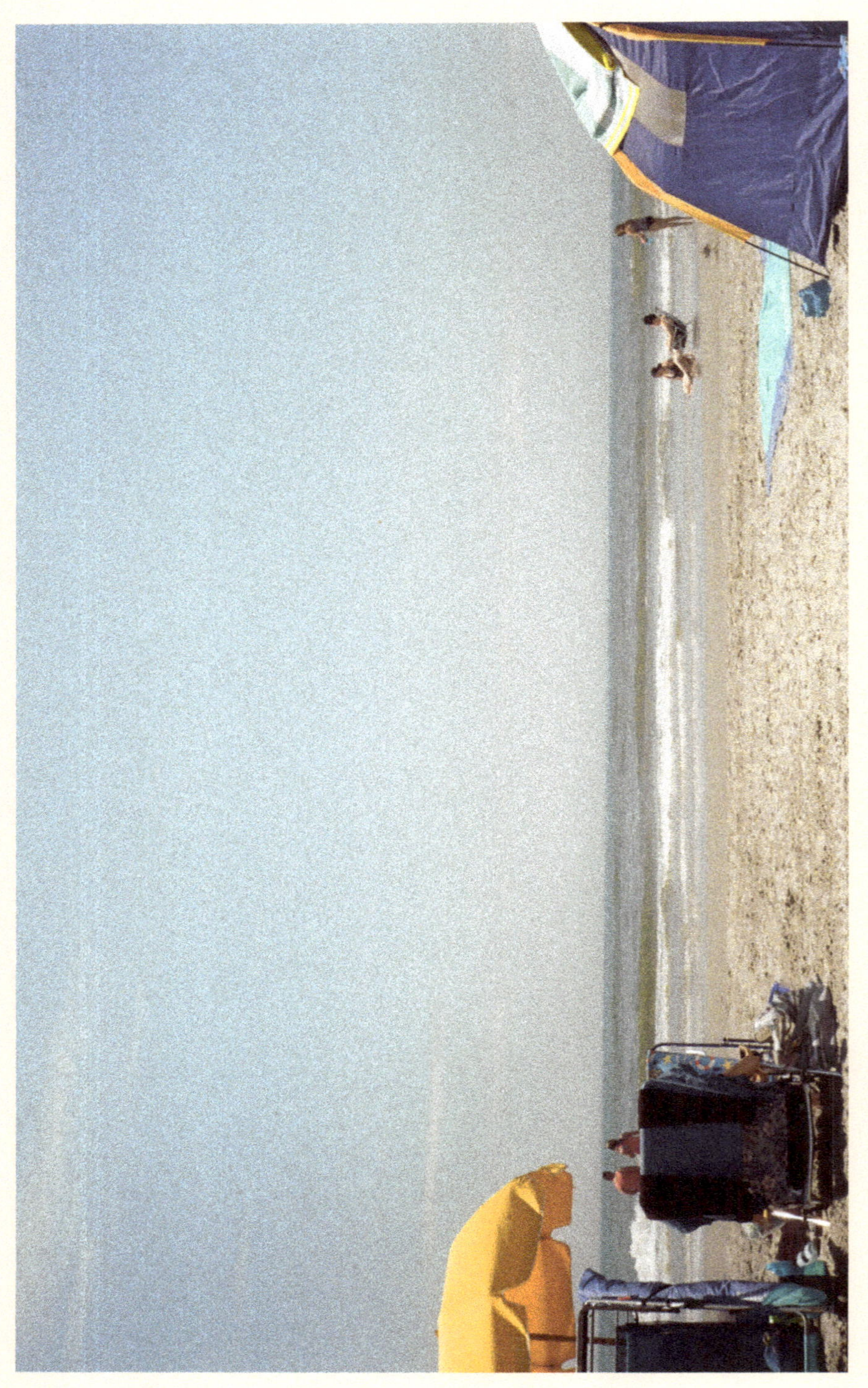

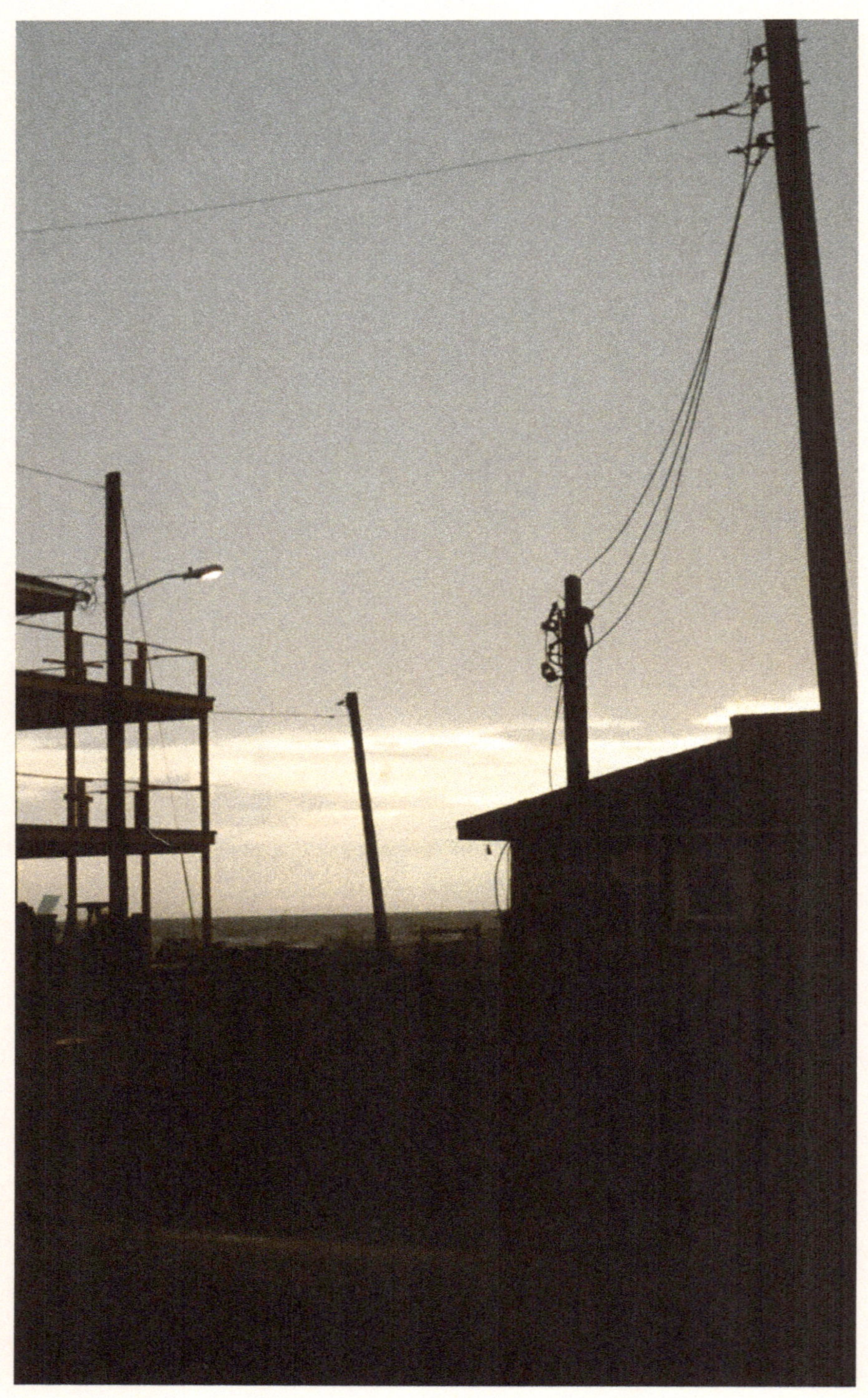

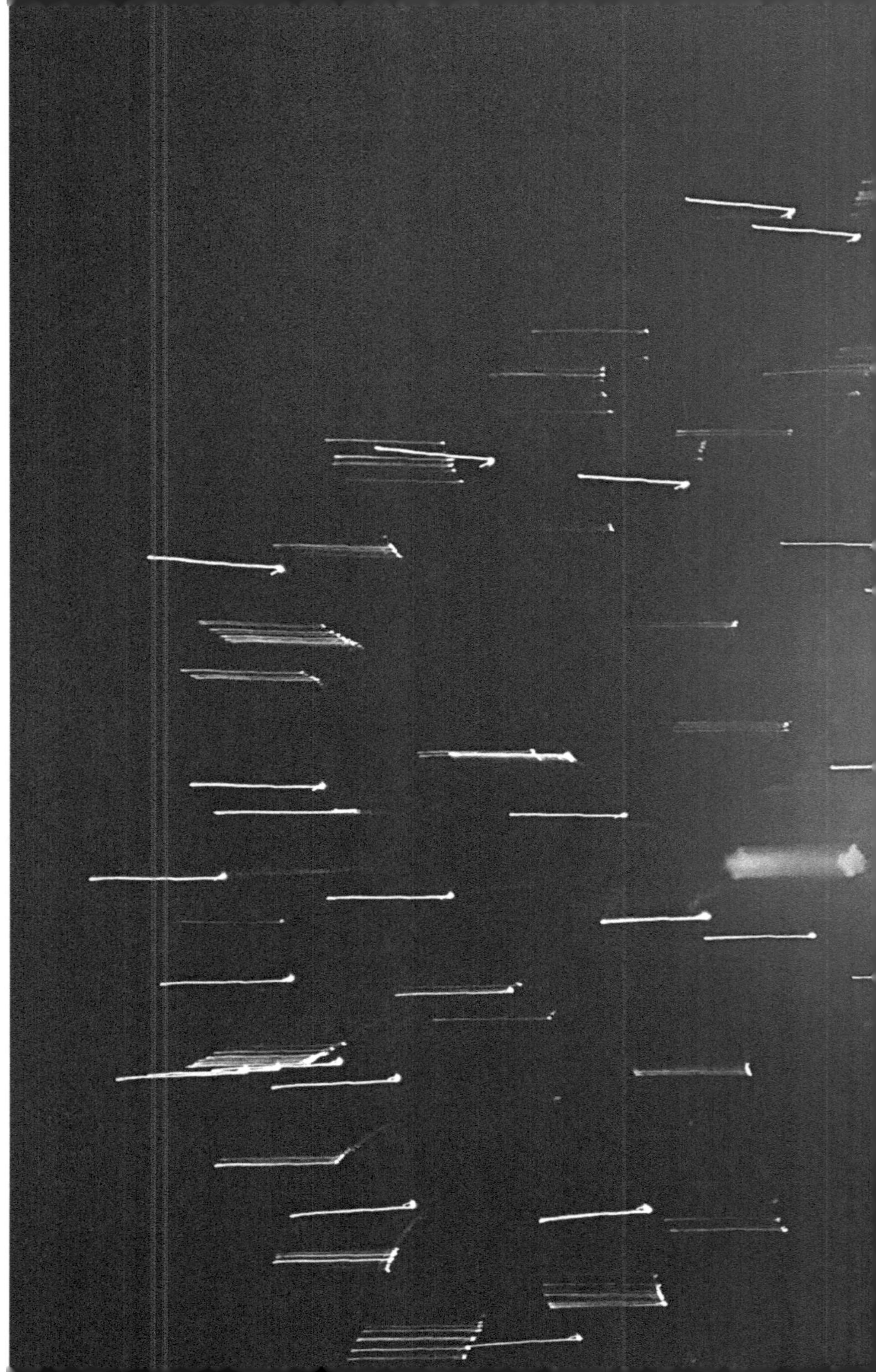